Pelican Book A706

The Geography of African Affairs

Paul Fordham was born in Norfolk in 1925 and went to the Friends School, Saffron Walden, for most of his schooldays. During and after the Second World War he spent some three and a half years as a 'Bevin-Boy' miner in Derbyshire. In 1950 he graduated in geography from Leeds University and, after brief spells as a tram conductor, jobbing gardener, and schoolmaster, spent the next ten years as a Resident Tutor in the Adult Education Department of Nottingham University, first in Lincolnshire and later in Derbyshire. As a result of over ten years in Derbyshire, he has come to look on it as his home.

While still at school, Paul Fordham read Julian Huxley's *Africa View* which first made him want to teach *about* Africa and, later, to teach *in* Africa. In 1961 he went to Makerere University College to be Resident Tutor in Buganda for the Extra-Mural Department, moving after a year to become Principal of the College of Social Studies (a residential college for adult education) at Kikuyu, in Kenya. In 1950 he married a fellow student and they have two sons.

The Geography of African Affairs

Paul Fordham

Penguin Books

BALTIMORE · MARYLAND

916
F

Penguin Books Ltd, Harmondsworth, Middlesex, England
Penguin Books Inc., 3300 Clipper Mill Road, Baltimore 11, Md, U.S.A.
Penguin Books Pty Ltd, Ringwood, Victoria, Australia

Published in Pelican Books 1965

Made and printed in Great Britain by
C. Nicholls & Company Ltd
Set in Monotype Plantin

28674

Contents

Part II – Regional Studies

WEST AFRICA

CENTRAL AFRICA

EAST AFRICA

SOUTHERN AFRICA

Preface

Anyone who has the effrontery to deal with so vast a subject in so small a compass must needs offer a convincing explanation for doing so.

Africa is large, its problems complex, and their solution increasingly pressing. Britain will continue to have a direct responsibility for some of these solutions and an indirect responsibility for most of the others – and yet most people seem to lack that basic geographical knowledge about the continent which is an essential beginning for any sensible appraisal of political issues.

In my teaching of University Adult Education Classes in England I found a need for such a book as this. I have not sought to write a complete Geography of Africa. What I have tried to do is to select from the whole mass of geographical facts about Africa south of the Sahara such information as seems important for an understanding of current political and economic problems. In doing this I have had in mind both the interested layman and those students of Geography who may wish to read a little farther than the normal confines of their subject.

The basic information and many of the ideas have been sifted from the writings of experts in a number of different fields. I hope that those who may be stimulated by this book will turn to them for further guidance.

Most of the sources used should be available on request from any good public library. They have been chosen with an eye both to availability and usefulness. The notes at the end of each chapter should therefore be regarded as a first guide to further reading. Statistics have been taken largely from the standard statistical reference books available in the larger reference libraries. The most useful sources of this kind are the *U.N. Statistical Yearbook*, the *U.N. Yearbook of International Trade Statistics*, and *The Statesman's Yearbook*.

My thanks to Mr and Mrs G. H. Moore, Mr A. H. Thornton, Mr H. C. Wiltshire, and my wife for many helpful suggestions and corrections and much-needed encouragement.

Makerere University College, Uganda.

June 1962.   P.E.F.

Delay in publication has made it possible to revise some of the text and statistical tables and to incorporate new data not previously available.

College of Social Studies, Kikuyu, Kenya.

July 1964.   P.E.F.

List of Tables

List of Maps

Part 1 A General Survey

1 A Land to Live in

If you were asked what sort of mental picture you have of the land of Africa you would probably reply that it was hot; possibly you would add that it was wet, and you might even go on to talk of jungle, wild animals, and unpleasant insects. On the other hand, if you have knowledge of people who have lived in one or another of the 'white settler' countries, you might have a quite different mental picture. You might talk then of summer all the year round, fertile soils, wonderful sunshine and spectacular scenery. In either case you would be describing a part as if it were the whole, forgetting Africa's truly continental scale. For Africa *is* a continent, and a very large one at that.

To say that Africa is 5,000 miles long from north to south and some 2,000 miles wide even at its narrowest point, gives the true measure of the distances involved. These measurements really come to life when one compares this size with countries which may be more familiar. (Map 1.) Can India really be as small as that? A huge country of nearly 400 million people, itself the greater part of what is known as a 'sub-continent'? Of course it is not India which is small: it is simply dwarfed by its much bigger surroundings. Even 'little' states like Ghana compare favourably in size with England and Wales while some, like Sudan, approach the size of India itself. Countries of this size are likely to contain a great variety of environments within their own borders, quite apart from the greater variety to be found in the continent as a whole. This variety will be considered in subsequent chapters, but size has other consequences too.

In countries which are technically backward and where communications have not been well developed, the larger the size of the territory the greater the problems of government will be. All governments have to exercise a minimum of physical control

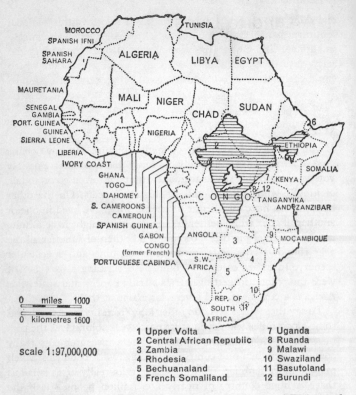

1 Upper Volta	7 Uganda
2 Central African Republic	8 Ruanda
3 Zambia	9 Malawi
4 Rhodesia	10 Swaziland
5 Bechuanaland	11 Basutoland
6 French Somaliland	12 Burundi

MAP I. The size of Africa, compared with England and Wales, and with India (without Kashmir)

and operate a workable administrative system or else they cease to govern (as the government of the Congo Republic ceased to govern in the summer of 1960). If they are authoritarian and have sufficient force at their disposal they may solve the problem as the Belgians did in the Congo by establishing an efficient system of airfields, strategically placed paratroops – and a monopoly of aeroplanes. If they wish to remain in any sense democratic, however, their authority must derive from a working minimum of popular consent, and for this there must be a working minimum of political cohesion (or 'solidarity' or 'national sentiment') throughout the entire country. This is the real difficulty. Apart from the educated minority this national sentiment hardly exists and has to be created. Even in a relatively small state like Ghana the government had to contend in the early days of independence with an official opposition which was a coalition of tribal interests rather than dissidents loyal to the new nation as a whole. In these circumstances the government found itself defending and promoting national solidarity with methods which may have seemed 'undemocratic'.

The difficulty over political cohesion in new states as big and diverse as those of Africa is largely one of the present. When it has been overcome, size becomes an advantage rather than a hindrance. For, except in a few overcrowded areas like parts of Kenya or Nigeria, there is room to expand and develop; room for the population to grow (as it is beginning to grow) and be absorbed; room to contain a growing and much needed labour force; room to experiment with new agricultural techniques to produce the food for the next generation as well as the food for today; above all, there will be room to live, as economic development in overcrowded lands frequently produces new troubles as well as solving old ones. 'A million peasants can dwell happily where a thousand car owners would chafe in frustration.'[1] Africa is fortunate to the degree that this is not her problem. One of the attractions for the Europeans who have settled there has been the space for work, travel, and leisure. This space will remain one of Africa's greatest assets for a long time to come.

PHYSICAL ENVIRONMENT

There are few who would deny that before this century Africa was – in the Western, technical, sense – the most backward of all the continents. This does not imply that nothing worthwhile came out of Africa before the Europeans arrived. There was a great deal that was worth while, about much of which we are still largely ignorant.[2] But, in comparison with the great civilizations of Asia, Europe, and the Americas, Africa does appear to have lagged behind in *material* achievements, and it is of more than academic interest to speculate on the possible reasons for this. There are those who would attempt to justify racial discrimination on the grounds of some 'innate inferiority' belonging to native Africans, an inferiority deduced from the assumption that they have not 'achieved' anything. Almost all reasonable men in the twentieth century consider this explanation absurd. What we can say is that there are certain aspects of Africa's physical environment which *by themselves* would account for any backwardness which Europeans found there.

First and foremost is the aspect of isolation. Most of us are what we are because of what we learn from our family, our friends, our neighbours, our enemies, and, above all, what we learn from the experience of the past. Most of us are content to learn, to imitate, to adapt, but not to invent. This process of learning and the accumulation of knowledge thrives on contact with other peoples and other ways of life, and stagnates in isolation. It is remarkable how all the really primitive peoples who survived into the nineteenth and twentieth centuries did so in extreme isolation and by adaptation to environments into which no other peoples were able or thought it profitable to penetrate. The Bushmen of the Kalahari Desert, the Australian and Tasmanian aborigines, and the 'Indians' along the southern tip of South America are examples which spring immediately to mind. Most Africans were not as isolated as this, but they were cut off to a large extent from contacts with the outside world. In the days before the European conquest of the seas, the Sahara desert constituted a considerable barrier to communications,* and right down to the nineteenth century there were other barriers which militated against effective, constructive contact.

RELIEF

In Relief, Africa is a vast plateau surface, with narrow coastal plains. The plateau is divided into a series of smaller plateau surfaces of different heights, often with abrupt edges both at the rim of the continent and at places in the interior. Land is higher in the south (where it averages 3,000 ft) than in the north (where it falls away to about 1,000 ft). Although generally flat and monotonous it is characterized by large shallow depressions, some of which form what the geographer calls 'basins of inland drainage' whose rivers end in inland lakes and swamps.

*But see pp. 97–9 below for medieval trans-Saharan contacts.

One further physical feature of note is the Great Rift Valley system of east Africa, of which the Red Sea forms part. The whole system is some 4,000 miles long and up to 100 miles wide, producing great local variations in relief, climate and vegetation. It contains most of the great lakes of east Africa, and the giant

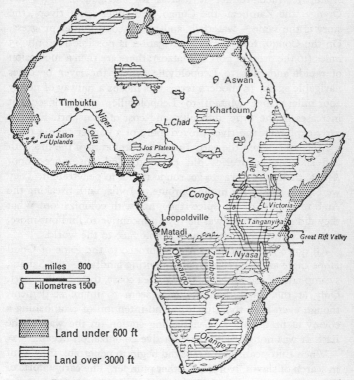

MAP 2. Relief and drainage (simplified)

volcanoes along its edges, with which are associated some of the continent's most fertile soils.

The edge of the plateau is always steep, sometimes spectacularly so, as with the Drakensberg in South Africa. It is these steep edges to the plateau which have contributed so much to isolation. For early explorers the easiest way to penetrate a new

land is to sail or paddle up the rivers – these are the natural lines
of communication. But in Africa not one of them is navigable
very far from the sea. They all 'fall off the edge' of the continent.
The Nile, the most obvious entry into the continent, is famous
for its cataracts, and farther south for its floating vegetation and
swamps, which render it useless for navigation. With the
Orange, the Zambezi, the Congo, and other great rivers, the
story is the same – waterfalls and rapids soon hinder progress.
On the Congo, for example, navigation is possible for only 85
miles (to the present port of Matadi); there are then a succession
of rapids and falls to Leopoldville, where the river becomes
navigable again. In modern terms this means a railway of nearly
200 miles from Matadi to Leopoldville, with consequent
increases in the time, difficulty, and cost of transport. For the
early explorers, the river proved more of a barrier than a path.

Moreover, when the early European explorers of the fifteenth
and sixteenth centuries did begin to find out more about
Africa, their object was to get round it, not to penetrate it. They
were concerned with finding a route to India, with breaking the
Arab monopoly of the spice trade, not with colonization. What
they did see of Africa was hardly an incentive to find out more,
for Africa turns her most inhospitable face to the world.

All down the west coast from Morocco to the Cape of Good
Hope there are a succession of uninviting landfalls – the Sahara,
swamp and dense forest on the Guinea coast, the Namib desert.
Only at the Cape does the land seem to invite settlement,
though even here the Dutch had no intention of establishing a
colony at first, only a re-victualling station on the way to the
East. It was not until 1685 that active colonization began.

When Europeans and Arabs did begin to penetrate, they went
in search of slaves, ivory, and other plunder. The early efforts of
the Portuguese to 'civilize' and Christianize in the Congo area[3]
gave way in the seventeenth century to the sort of destructive
contact which became characteristic of all European penetration
for over 200 years. This contact was not of the kind to provide a
release from isolation and a stimulus to new effort and growth.
Inwards from the extreme south and north, isolation remained
an important aspect of African life until this century.

In addition to isolation there were other aspects of great

difficulty which were presented to man by his physical environment. Difficulties are not always a disadvantage. They may be a desirable, even a necessary, stimulus to civilization. With Toynbee one may say that,

Ease is inimical to civilization ... The greater the ease of the environment, the weaker the stimulus towards civilization.[4]

or agree with Burke, that

... difficulty ... has been the glory of all the great masters in all the arts to confront and to overcome; and when they had overcome the first difficulty, to turn it into an instrument for new conquests over new difficulties ...[5]

Nevertheless there must come a point when the stimulus provided by difficulty becomes instead a crushing burden. This has certainly been true of the physical environment in Africa.

CLIMATE

The Climate in its direct effects on human beings has often been stressed, perhaps over-stressed. There are few parts of Africa where the climate is debilitating for human beings all the year round, and even in these areas the pith helmet and the spine pad are things of the past. What is increasingly realized is that the *indirect* effects of climate, particularly on water supply, soils, and disease, are of much greater significance in human terms. It is these which have been barriers to human progress in the past and which can only now be overcome with the technical aids of the twentieth century.

The climates of Africa possess three significant aspects. First, the continent's position about the equator determines the equatorial or tropical nature of most of its climates. Only the extreme north and the extreme south lie outside the tropics, and there are few places anywhere in the continent where plant growth is ever checked by cold. This occurs only in the highest mountain areas.

Secondly, because most of the continent is at least 1,000 ft and often considerably more above sea level, there are very few places in Black Africa where temperature is excessively high. Only along the west coast, the Congo basin, and the coastal strip of east Africa are there mean annual temperatures of over 80 degrees – temperatures which, especially when combined with high humidities, are generally agreed to be rather enervating.

Thirdly, water rather than temperature is the critical factor. Water shortage is perhaps the most important limiting factor of

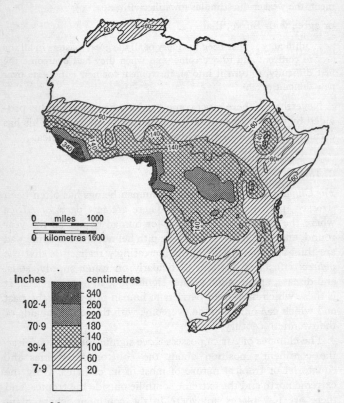

Inches		centimetres
		340
102·4		260
		220
		180
70·9		140
		100
39·4		60
7·9		20

MAP 3. Mean annual rainfall

the physical environment today, for 'water is scanty in at least three quarters of Africa south of the Sahara'.[6] Around the equator, where no month is really dry (except in parts of Kenya) and there are generally two rain maxima in spring and autumn, there is not generally a water problem. Very rapidly, however, as you move away from the equator, these two rain maxima merge into one rainy season (summer), the length of this season grows, and the amount and reliability of the rainfall steadily decrease.

Water is put to many and varied uses in modern society. As the standard of living rises, so does the standard of sanitation, plumbing, and the consequent consumption of water. The creation of industry brings many problems in its train, not least of which is the consumption of water. Conservation of water for industrial use is already a serious problem on the Witwatersrand in South Africa.[7]

Fisheries, both natural and artificial, are likely to play an increasingly important part in an Africa still chronically short of enough protein foods. All these, as well as the demands of irrigation, transport and water power, will have to be met in the Africa of the future.

With the exception of South West Africa, Bechuanaland, the Sahara, and parts of Tanganyika and Kenya, there is enough total rainfall over the whole of inter-tropical Africa. It is the unreliability of the amount and the length of the dry season which constitute the problems. Methods of control must aim to reduce or eliminate the run-off of water, to allow its gradual use throughout the dry season.

SOILS

The poverty of soils in tropical Africa has been a hindrance to agriculture in most areas. Any advanced civilization must rest on the production of a food surplus, but if everyone is struggling to produce enough (or less than enough) to eat, there will be little time and opportunity for that division of labour so essential to the accumulation of material wealth.

It used to be thought, because so much of tropical Africa is covered with luxuriant vegetation, that the underlying soils must necessarily be rich. Only remove this dense plant cover, it was argued, and fertile agricultural land would be revealed. We now know that this is not so. In the wetter areas, soils under tropical forest wear out very rapidly when the land is cleared. Such land must be left fallow again for long periods at a time unless some artificial methods of regeneration are applied. 'Tropical soils are poorer and more fragile than those of temperate regions. Great

care is needed in using them, if their further destruction and
impoverishment are to be avoided. These conditions give
tropical agriculture a precarious character which is absent from
the temperate belt.'[8]

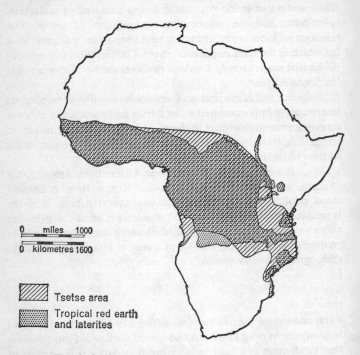

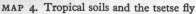

    0   miles   1000

    0   kilometres 1600

Tsetse area

Tropical red earth
and laterites

MAP 4. Tropical soils and the tsetse fly

The answer to the apparent paradox of luxuriant vegetation
on poor soil is that the tropical forest lives in a state of equilibrium with itself and takes very little nourishment from the soil.
For parts of the Congo it has been estimated that between 20 and
25 tons of leaves and branches fall on each acre every year. This
enormous quantity of organic material quickly decomposes
under the prevailing climatic conditions and forms the humus
and salts on which the trees directly feed. But it never becomes
part of more than the top few inches of soil. Once you clear away

the trees, you destroy the equilibrium, and the soil is revealed in all its actual poverty.

This general poverty of tropical soils is caused by the climate under which they are formed. Myriads of insects (especially termites) which flourish in the hot, wet areas, begin the decomposition of organic matter. These, together with the countless micro-organisms, soon convert the branches and leaves into humus and the humus into soluble salts. If they are not used within a few weeks of their formation, they are washed away (or 'leached') by the heavy rain. Tropical soils are thus poor in plant foods, and highly acid because any available lime is soon leached away, while the rapid conversion of humus into soluble salts prevents the storage of these salts for use by cultivated plants. Even the application of manure has an effect over months rather than the years enjoyed by temperate soils.

Experiments have shown that the activity of micro-organisms in decomposing humus is increased fairly rapidly by a rise in the average temperature. In Java, the 'humus content of the surface layer of the soil was shown to rise from 5 per cent at an altitude of 1,000 feet above sea level and a mean annual temperature of 76 degrees F. to 14 per cent at an altitude of 3,250 feet and a mean temperature of 68 degrees F.'[9] This range of temperature is about the same as the difference between much of Uganda and the tropical coast lands of east Africa. Away from the higher parts of the east African plateau, mean annual temperatures in tropical Africa are well above 70 degrees F. The only tropical soils which are naturally fertile are those which have not yet had time to become poor – those formed from fairly recent non-acid volcanic ash, as in parts of east Africa on the margins of the Rift Valleys, or those derived from recent river alluvium, as in a few small areas near the coasts. Only the Nile Valley in the north provided any comparable natural fertility with the great river valleys of south and east Asia.

Two further problems accentuate the poverty of African soils: soil erosion and lateritization.

Soil erosion, 'a malignant form of a natural phenomenon',[10] is essentially a man-made problem. Leave the soil with its natural protective plant cover, either forest or grassland, and malignant erosion does not occur; but once this cover is removed, the opportunities for wind and rain to do damage are greatly increased. Bush clearance by burning, the unthinking transference of European methods and tools to an African environment, and overgrazing have all contributed to the exposure of African soils and their removal by wind and rain.

Unless ploughing is always done by following the contours, the furrow becomes a gulley after a tropical deluge, and a gulley which becomes deeper and wider with each downpour. Lack of humus in the soil reduces its rate of water absorption, with a consequent increase in the rate of run-off and removal of top soil. In the dry season, soil reduced to a powder can quickly and drama-tically be removed either by wind or by the next heavy rain. It is, in fact, in the drier areas that the problem is at its most acute, and these are just the areas which have some of the best soils in Africa. As you move out of the area of poor soils, you move into the areas where erosion and poor water supply are of increasing significance.

Most of the red soils of the tropics are lateritic to a greater or lesser extent. Pure laterite, described by Gourou as a 'pedological leprosy'[11] and 'utterly infertile'[12] is a rock rather than a soil. Roads can be made of it as well as buildings, and it stands up to weathering rather better than some rocks. It is composed of the hydroxides of iron and aluminium in various proportions, is formed as the end product in the creation of soil from other rocks under tropical conditions, and in its pure form contains absolutely nothing that plants can absorb.

In areas with a dry season, laterite forms as a hard crust on the surface of the land. During the dry season, water percolates upwards, bringing with it in solution the hydroxides of iron and aluminium which are deposited at the surface as a hard pan or crust. In those areas which have no significant dry season, as in the Congo Basin, the laterite forms at a depth varying from 18 inches to 9 feet, but even here it may quickly be exposed if the processes of man-induced soil erosion get to work.

Laterite is a dead soil, a rock which does not decompose and on which chemical erosion has no effect. Areas whose surface is formed by laterite are worthless. Soils in which laterite is incompletely formed may be cultivated if they offer a good physical texture, as in certain

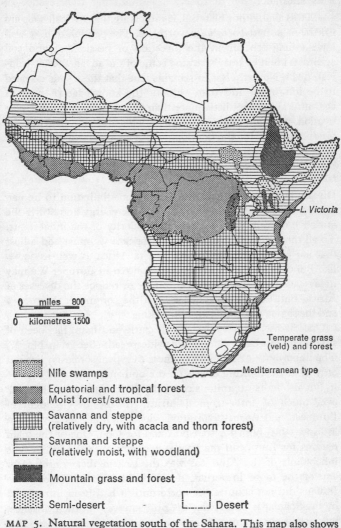

L. Victoria

Temperate grass
(veld) and forest

Mediterranean type

Nile swamps

Equatorial and tropical forest
Moist forest/savanna

Savanna and steppe
(relatively dry, with acacia and thorn forest)

Savanna and steppe
(relatively moist, with woodland)

Mountain grass and forest

Semi-desert   Desert

MAP 5. Natural vegetation south of the Sahara. This map also shows political boundaries. (For greater detail see R. W. J. Keay, *Vegetation Map of Africa*, 1959)

gritty soils observed in the lower Congo valley; but they are very poor nevertheless.[13]

All this should not be taken as indicating that African soils are for the most part *potentially* worthless. The pendulum may well have swung too far in the direction of pessimism, and soil scientists are now busy stressing some of the advantages of tropical soils.[14] Nevertheless, it remains true that these soils do need to be improved, and that, without the knowledge of modern agricultural science, little more than the prevailing shifting cultivation was possible in the past. This did not provide the productive base for the development of an advanced civilization.

DISEASE

Disease has certainly constituted a serious limitation to human activity in Africa. Even today it saps the energy and stifles the initiative of millions – perhaps the majority of the inhabitants. To all those diseases familiar to Europeans we must add a host that are peculiar to the tropics and to Africa as well as some, like Bubonic Plague, now almost forgotten in Europe. We may today have the knowledge to eliminate or reduce the diseases of Africa, but, as with so much else in the continent, the money and the skilled personnel are still lacking.

One disease, which affects both cattle and man, has been of supreme importance and is still widespread. (See Map No. 4.) The importance of sleeping sickness (Trypanosomiasis) lies not only in its debilitating effects on the human beings who survive it, but also in its calamitous consequence for the rearing of stock over much of inter-tropical Africa. In the development of European and Asian civilizations domestic animals have been indispensable, both for transport and for food. One of the main reasons for European material superiority over the indigenous inhabitants of the Americas was the lack in that continent of any of the more important domesticable animals (the Plains Indians did not acquire the horse until it had been introduced by the Spaniards). In Africa the problem was not their absence, but lack of opportunity to rear and maintain healthy stock. The effect on material achievements was the same.

Today it is possible to combat sleeping sickness both by

TABLE I

No. of medical practitioners in selected countries
(1958 unless otherwise stated.)

Country	No. of doctors	No. of inhabitants per doctor
Angola	226 (1959)	20,000
Basutoland	32	21,000
Cameroun	109 (1959)	37,000
Ghana	186 (1955)	36,000
Kenya	607	*13,000
Liberia	62 (1956)	20,000
Nigeria	958 (1959)	35,000
Rhodesia	619	*5,000
Malawi	71	40,000
Ruanda and Burundi	89	50,000
Uganda	377	18,000
Republic of South Africa	7,354 (1957)	2,000
U.K.	50,178	1,000
India	76,916 (1956)	56,000

*Figures for countries having large numbers of non-Africans cannot really be compared with those having only small numbers of non-Africans. In the former, doctors generally serve the non-African community, and the number of African inhabitants per doctor may still be enormous.

SOURCE: *United Nations Statistical Yearbook 1961*, Tables 1 and 177.

immunizing animals and man and by the clearance of bush, the breeding ground of the tsetse fly which carries the disease. The fly cannot maintain itself in completely open country, such as that cleared for cultivation, or in dense forest. Both immunization and bush clearance are expensive, however, and the final elimination of sleeping sickness will depend on how much money is made available for the job.

There are several ways of classifying African diseases – according to the way they are spread, their causative organisms, or the way of life pursued by their human sufferers.[15] This last seems the most sensible way for this study and is the one adopted here. Using it, we can establish four main categories.

The first contains all those diseases especially associated with the primitive rural life – still the lot of most of Africa's peoples. These are diseases spread mainly (though not entirely) by the insect carriers of disease, and they will only be eliminated or reduced in importance with improved housing, water supply, and generally improved standards of hygiene. They include malaria, sleeping sickness, yellow fever, and pneumonia.

The second group are those specifically associated with insanitary conditions and habits, some of which have become more prevalent as Europeans have encouraged the greater movement and mixing of peoples, crowding into urban slums, and also as clothing habits have changed. 'Dirty clothes are a poor substitute for clean nudity.'[16] They include plague, typhus, leprosy, various worm parasites and bilharziasis.

The third group are those whose spread is mainly due to ignorance, like the venereal diseases and yaws, a disease whose symptoms are very similar to those of syphilis, but which is spread from infected cuts and to which young children are particularly prone.

The fourth group are the diseases due to malnutrition, of which kwashiorkor has received most attention in recent years. The name is used for a complex of symptoms associated with severe malnutrition, especially protein deficiency, a complex which affects large numbers of children just after weaning, when they are put on to a diet consisting almost entirely of starchy food. In 'certain parts of Africa it is probable that the majority of the children in the second and third year of life suffer from kwashiorkor.'[17] Among the symptoms are retarded growth, swollen bellies, and permanent damage to the liver and possibly other organs. There is also a death rate of at least 30 per cent. In later life the high incidence of cirrhosis and cancer of the liver is thought to be due to childhood kwashiorkor. 'In England it is often said that a man is as old as his arteries. In tropical Africa it would seem to be more true to say that a man is as old as his liver.'[18]

In one sense we might place most of Africa's diseases in the last category, because they are nearly all of them aggravated by the prevalent malnutrition. A pioneer study in this field was that of Orr and Gilks, in 1931, on the Masai and Kikuyu tribes of Kenya.[19] The Masai live on a diet of milk, meat, and raw blood, one which is unusually high in protein, fats and calcium. The Kikuyu live mainly on cereals, roots, and fruit, one more nearly typical of most of Africa. It was found that the average male Masai was 5 inches taller, 23 lb heavier, and had a muscular strength 50 per cent greater than his Kikuyu counterpart. Disease among the Kikuyu was much more prevalent, especially bone deformities, dental caries, anaemia, pulmonary conditions, and tropical ulcer. Among the Masai only rheumatoid arthritis and intestinal stasis were more prevalent than among the Kikuyu. The improvement of health in Africa is to a large extent a question of improving diets.

Possibilities for the future development of Africa will be considered in Chapter 5, and the fact that past and present difficulties have been emphasized here does not mean that they cannot be overcome. Isolation has probably been the most important factor making for backwardness in the past, and the difficulties of the environment could not be effectively challenged until this isolation had been overcome. Much of the initial conquest by Europeans did not stimulate Africans to greater achievements, it merely added to their burdens. It is only now, in the middle of the twentieth century, that Africans have both the opportunity to develop on their own, and knowledge of the outside world to help them do so. Africa is still a land of difficulties, but they need not remain the crushing burdens that they have been in the past. They can now take their place with those of Burke as a stimulus to further effort. The test of the 'innate capacity' of Africans lies in the future and not in the past.

Even when talking of the past we should be wary of judging purely from a European standpoint. It is true that on the level of material culture much of Africa was in the early 'iron age' and there were areas more primitive even than that. There was, however, some elaborate social and political organization, especially in west Africa, while the influence of African art and music on that of Europe has been profound and far-reaching during the course of this century. Perhaps we may allow the last word to one of Africa's most primitive stone-age men, a Bushman from the Kalahari Desert:

'What is considered the worst thing a man can do?' I once asked Tsonoma (the Medicine Man). He answered, without hesitation, that the gravest offence was to fight with someone else in the clan. It was considered unworthy and stupid. For that reason a boy who showed signs of aggressiveness was closely watched by all the adults and taken out on long, tough hunting trips to learn sense and discipline. In their legends, there are no heroes who attain distinction by force of arms . . .[20]

Notes on Chapter 1

1. R. A. Piddington, *The Limits of Mankind*, 1956, p.2.
2. Basil Davidson, *Old Africa Rediscovered*, 1959.
3. See J. Duffy, *Portuguese Africa*, 1959, Chap. 1.
4. *Study of History*, Vol. 2, 1934.
5. *Reflections on the Revolution in France*, World Classics edn., pp. 184–5.
6. E. B. Worthington, *Science in the Development of Africa*, 1958, p. 114.
7. See Chapter 12 below.
8. P. Gourou. *The Tropical World*, 2nd edn, 1958, p. 13.
9. ibid., p. 17.
10. L. D. Stamp, *Africa*, 1953, p. 101.
11. ibid., p. 21.
12. ibid., p. 20.
13. ibid., p. 22.
14. E. B. Worthington, op. cit., p. 140.
15. The Approach of E. B. Worthington.
16. E. B. Worthington, op. cit., p. 360.
17. J. C. Carothers, *The African Mind in Health and Disease*, W.H.O., 1953, p. 71.
18. ibid., p. 71.
19. J. Boyd Orr and J. D. Gilks, *The Physique and Health of Two African Tribes*.
20. J. Bjerre, *Kalahari*, 1960, p. 110.

SUGGESTIONS FOR FURTHER READING

As well as those books mentioned above:
W. G. Kendrew, *The Climates of the Continents*, 1953 (Chapter 5).

D. H. K. Lee, *Climate and Economic Development in the Tropics*, 1957.

E. Huntington, *Mainsprings of Civilization*, 1945.

G. V. Jacks and R. O. Whyte, *The Rape of the Earth*, 1949.

Appendix to Chapter 1

Some Notes on the Principal Diseases of Tropical Africa

DISEASES PARTICULARLY ASSOCIATED WITH PRIMITIVE RURAL LIFE

They are likely to disappear or be reduced in importance only with improved housing, sanitation, and water supply – i.e. greater insulation from the wild environment. They include in particular those diseases carried by biting winged insects.

Malaria. Now being reduced in a systematic campaign conducted by W.H.O. (World Health Organization) against the malarial mosquito.

Yellow Fever. A disease of monkeys which occasionally assumes epidemic proportions in man. Transmitted by mosquitos. In a recent epidemic in Nigeria (1951) there were 600 deaths out of 5,500 cases.

Sleeping Sickness. Spread to animals and man by tsetse flies of various species. Methods of control include bush clearance (to eliminate flies), destruction of wild game (to eliminate tolerant animal hosts) and the immunization of domestic animals and man. Immunization lasts only six months.

Onchocersiasis. Infestation by filarial worm and transmitted by a fly which lives near rivers and streams – hence the name *River Blindness* which is applied to the condition which often develops.

Pneumonia and Tuberculosis, common causes of death among Africans, may also be included in this category.

DISEASES PRIMARILY DUE TO INSANITARY CONDITIONS AND HABITS

Some of these are an increasing problem due to the movement of people into overcrowded towns and cities.

Trachoma. Very high infection rates often leading to partial or total blindness. Antibiotics are effective.

Typhus. Both louse-borne and flea-borne varieties.

Typhoid Fever and intestinal infections especially prevalent in urban slums.

Hookworm. Infestation is high. Live in the small intestine, taking blood from the host. Common cause of anaemia and general debility. Easy to treat but re-infestation is usual.

Plague. Spread by fleas and still occurs, though speedy control is possible.

Relapsing Fever, both tick-borne and louse-borne, is another herd disease which sometimes assumes epidemic proportions. *Leprosy* might come either in this or the next category. Although still a serious problem, it is not in fact easy to catch and usually occurs only after long contact with an infected person. Segregation and treatment may eventually eliminate this disease.

DISEASES WHOSE DISSEMINATION IS MAINLY DUE TO IGNORANCE

The Venereal Diseases, of which Gonorrhoea is native to Africa and Syphilis has been imported. High infection rates especially for the former (80 per cent in some areas).

Yaws is closely related to Syphilis although not a venereal disease. It should probably come in the category of diseases associated with primitive rural life.

Bilharzia. Caused by a worm, the life cycle of which passes through man and certain species of water snail. Occurs in water and streams throughout tropical Africa. Debilitating, especially for the undernourished.

DIETARY DEFICIENCY DISEASES

Many of the diseases in the first three categories are made worse by the prevalent inadequate diets. Of the specific deficiency diseases, *Kwashiorkor* is the most important (see text), while *Tropical Ulcer* is also a serious problem in some areas.

2 Peoples and the Old Economic Order

RACES AND TRIBES

Most of those belonging to the broad racial division of mankind that the anthropologist calls 'Negroid' live in Africa; and, of those that do not, most have descended from the slaves sold out of Africa in the last 400 years. There is great variety within the Negroid group, but Africa south of the Sahara is essentially Negro in a way which is true of no other major part of the world.

Just where and when the Negro evolved we cannot say with any certainty. The origin of man in general and of the Negro in particular provides fascinating fields of speculation for the scholar and a confusing maze of conflicting theories for the layman. Most theories of man's origins have pictured a single centre of evolution from which men have moved outwards over thousands of years, later becoming differentiated into various racial types as a result of subsequent evolution in isolation from one another. Many have thought of South West Asia as the original home of mankind, but the archaeological discoveries of Leakey and others in east and south Africa suggest that the origins of man may lie in Africa rather than elsewhere. Which centre of origin is finally accepted depends on what is discovered in the future, and is unlikely to affect the generally accepted view that the area of differentiation of the Negro lies somewhere in Africa, probably in the west. The period during which the different human types became differentiated stretches back into remote pre-history, when it is likely that movement both into and out of the central and southern parts of the continent was much easier than today.

During the Pleistocene ice ages in Europe, the Sahara desert did not exist. Instead, northern Africa had a climate and vegetation not unlike that of Western Europe now, and there was no question of isolation from the rest of the Old World. It was only with the retreat northwards of the European ice sheets that the gradual drying out of the Sahara began, a process which probably first impeded human movement somewhere between 10,000 and 5,000 B.C. This period of Saharan desiccation coincided with the discovery of how to produce food by cultivation and the domestication of animals. These discoveries, particularly associated with the civilizations of ancient Egypt, Mesopotamia, and the Indus valley, probably spread south of the Sahara during the second or third millennium B.C.

Today the Sahara is the great human divide between Negro Africa to the south and Caucasoid* to the north: between the Africa which has been isolated and the Africa which has been in sustained contact with Europe and Asia. There has been some mixing along the fringes in the west and some more extensive inter-mixture in the east, especially in the southern Sudan, Ethiopia, Somalia, Kenya, and Uganda. Nevertheless, the Himalaya mountains[1] are the only other land barrier in the world across which there is such a contrast in 'racial' type.

'Racial' is placed in inverted commas because even in Africa the isolation of human groups has never been complete enough for long enough to permit of any racial 'purity' in the biological sense. As is the case elsewhere in the world, each group merges almost imperceptibly into its neighbours. Moreover, the exact knowledge required to make a proper classification of the races of Africa is not available, and we still have to rely on a classification which is based primarily on language and only to a lesser extent on physical features. Language is a poor criterion on which to rely, because languages spread farther and faster than the physical types which may have originated them. What follows should be regarded as the sort of generalization which may well have to be revised when the knowledge at our disposal has improved.

In the most remote, impenetrable and difficult areas live two groups of people whose physical distinctiveness and ways of life mark them out as peoples apart – the Pygmies of the Congo

*The Anthropologists' term for the huge group of mankind which stretches from Western Europe south-eastwards to India. It is perhaps best described as the 'White/Brown' race.

Basin and the Bushmen of the Kalahari Desert. Both have been pushed into their present homelands by the entry of materially more advanced peoples into the more favourable environments. Both are hunters and gatherers with a stone age culture, and both are probably doomed to extinction or absorption like other

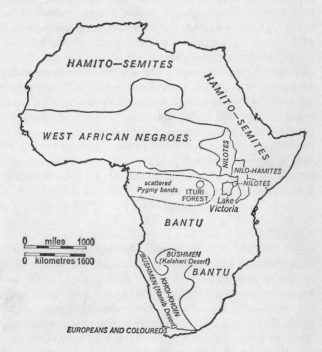

MAP 6. Major 'racial' groups in the 18th century. (Principal sources: J. H. Greenberg, *Studies in African Linguistic Classification*, 1955; I. Schapera, *The Khoisan Peoples of Southern Africa*, 1930)

primitive hunters before them. They are small in number (about 100,000 Pygmies and 50,000 Bushmen) but were undoubtedly more numerous and widespread in the past. Their present ways of life and small physique probably represent comparatively recent adaptations to the unfavourable environments into which they have retreated.[2]

Pygmies

The Pygmies are normally less than five feet tall, with arms very long in relation to their legs. Their skin is yellowish to dark brown and their bodies are covered with light downy hair. They have large prominent eyes, flat noses, and are generally progna-thous.* They live in small bands of about fifty individuals, hunt with bows and poisoned arrows, and gather berries and roots.

They have come to rely on the surrounding agricultural tribes with whom they exchange game and other forest products for cultivated foods. 'Almost nowhere today do Pygmies occupy independent tracts of land. Rather they are attached in small bands to particular Negro chiefs or headmen in a relationship which, though reciprocal, is clearly dependent . . .'.[3] Many of the Pygmies have been absorbed into these surrounding tribes and, where not absorbed, they have often adopted the agricul-tural life of their Negro neighbours. As far as is known, there is no distinct Pygmy language.

Bushmen

The Bushmen are a fascinating remnant group now confined to the Kalahari Desert and its margins but who were at one time or another found over the whole of Africa. We know this largely because of their skill as cave painters, for examples of their art have been found in the Sahara and in east Africa as well as in the south. That it is Bushmen art we are tolerably sure, not only on the grounds of style, but because of the depiction of people with one of the unique physical features of the Bushmen – an ex-aggerated inward curvature of the base of the spine and a fatty deposit on buttocks and thighs known as steatopygia.[4] Bushmen also use (together with the Khoi-Khoin or Hottentot) a distinc-tive type of language containing 'click' sounds, and traces of these, too, are still found among some east and south African tribes.[5]

The Bushmen are physically short (just over 5 feet), slender

*A term referring to the normal Negroid characteristic, whereby the face below the forehead, and especially the jaw, is projected forward.

in build, with yellow to brown skin and 'peppercorn' hair, the hair so tightly spiralled as to leave bare patches of skin showing between the 'peppercorns'. They have high cheek bones, flat noses, high and broad foreheads, and pointed chins. Their eyes are narrow and almond-shaped but not Mongoloid, and they are not prognathous except where they have intermixed with Negroes. Materially, they are like the Pygmies in leading a simple hunting life with bows and poisoned arrows, although unlike the Pygmies they are completely dependent on their own resourcefulness in a particularly harsh environment. Their social organization is extremely simple, and it is as artists that they have made their unique cultural contribution.

Apart from these remnant groups, Africa south of the Sahara is the homeland of various Negro peoples. In the west, cut off by the Sahara to the north, the sea to the south and a broad belt of forest to the south-east, there seems to have been least human movement. Here are found people who show in clearest form the physical features characteristic of the Negro. In the east, on the other hand, there has clearly been much more movement. The more open country to the east of the Nile swamps and west of the Ethiopian Highlands provides a narrow, if difficult, route between north and south, and as a result, the peoples of east, central, and southern Africa are much more variable in physical type.

West African Negroes

West African Negroes number about 60 million people. They are usually over five and a half feet tall,[6] with dark brown to black skin, spiralled but not 'peppercorn' hair, and broad flat noses. Their lips are usually fully everted and there is pronounced prognathism.

The West African Negroes are usually cultivators, with few cattle, and their true homeland is the savanna country away from the coast, although they have moved into the forest zone since about the beginning of the Christian era. Among the tribal groupings some of the better known are the Ashanti, centred on Kumasi in Ghana, and the Hausa, Yoruba, and Ibo of Nigeria.

In social and political organization and in the practice of the plastic arts West Africans were far advanced before the coming of Europeans to the coast. There were a number of highly organized states like Ashanti, Dahomey, and the Yoruba kingdoms, with elaborate military organization and complex legal systems. The artistic achievements of Benin and the Yoruba areas are well known, but all through the area woodworking, textiles, and craftsmanship in gold and silver were very highly developed.

Away from the west, most of central and southern Africa was probably occupied by Pygmy and Bushman hunters until after the beginning of the Christian era. Today it is occupied by various Negro groups, many of whom are significantly different in physical type from the Negroes of the west. There is great physical variety in both East and South Africa and signs in many areas of relatively recent and incomplete 'racial' mixture.

Hamites

The Hamites were at one time thought to be recent intruders into eastern and southern Africa and to have altered both the culture and physical type of the various Negro tribes that they found there. Recent archaeological research has now shown, however, that Caucasoid physical types have lived in east Africa for at least six or seven thousand years. The southward movement of these 'proto-Hamites'* into east Africa pre-dates by several thousand years the entry from the west of Bantu-speaking Negro cultivators.

These 'proto-Hamites' possibly account for the markedly Caucasoid physical features found in many of the tribes of east and southern Africa. Those groups amongst whom such features appear most common are pastoralists, until recently often forming a distinct caste ruling over their more numerous neighbours who live by cultivation. Examples of this dual cultural and social system are the Hima and Iru of Ankole in Uganda and the Tutsi and Hutu of Ruanda and Burundi. In the case of both the Hima and the Tutsi, narrow noses and faces make them physically as well as culturally distinct from their more Negroid neighbours. Many of the Hima and Tutsi feel a sense of superiority on account of this physical distinctiveness. Similar narrow noses

*So called by Leakey.

and faces can be observed in the ruling families of some other tribes, notably the Ganda in Uganda.

Nilo-Hamites and Nilotes

The Nilo-Hamites (about $1\frac{1}{2}$ million) and the Nilotes (about 10 million) are distinguished mainly on linguistic but partly also on cultural grounds. They live in parts of the southern Sudan, Kenya, and northern Tanganyika, and most of them are pastoralists, either nomadic or semi-nomadic. Some groups have adopted the more sedentary life of their Bantu neighbours, like the Nilo-Hamitic Nandi and Nilotic Luo of western Kenya. Many of the Nilotes, notably in the southern Sudan, are distinguished by their tall stature and extreme long-headedness.

Bantu

The Bantu, numbering some 60 million people, are much the most important group of Negroes outside the West, covering almost the whole of Africa south of about 5 degrees north latitude. Like the other two groups they are separated on linguistic rather than racial grounds, although most are physically distinct from West Africans. In the east, and especially in the south, they are neither so dark nor so prognathous, but in the north and west the differences are less marked.

The Bantu have spread out into most of the lands they now occupy only within the last 2,000 years, and much of their occupancy is clearly more recent that that. There is some difference of opinion as to where they originated, but the linguistic evidence points to the area of the Cameroon highlands.[7] Bantu languages are so closely related that their present wide dispersal is likely to have been a relatively recent one. 'As little as 2,000 years ago Bantu may have been a single language spoken in an area much smaller than that occupied today by its descendants. . . .'[8] In any event they would have been unable to colonize the forest zone in such large numbers until they had acquired imported food plants (see pp. 49–52 below), and one writer[9] has placed their entry into the Congo rain forest as late as the seventeenth century.

Most of the eastern and southern Bantu combine cultivation (a woman's job) with cattle keeping (the prerogative of the men). Only where the existence of the tsetse fly prevents effective stock-rearing are cattle absent. In the west, a forest environment confines them to cultivation.

Khoi-Khoin (Hottentots)

Khoi-Khoin (Hottentots), numbering about 24,000 today, are physically and linguistically more akin to the Bushmen than other groups, but, being pastoralists, are culturally quite distinct. They are taller and more prognathous than Bushmen and are usually regarded as a cross between Bushmen and proto-Hamites, perhaps originating in the Great Lakes region and migrating southwards with their cattle to their present habitat. They help to form the present Cape Coloured population, and the lighter skins of the southern Bantu may be accounted for by mixture with them.

SUBSISTENCE ECONOMIES

Types of Economy

With the exception of the pastoral Nilotes, Nilo-Hamites and Khoi-Khoin, and a few hunting and fishing peoples, the great majority of Africans – outside the industrial areas of southern Africa – are engaged in agriculture or in agriculture combined with pastoralism. Even where the reverence for cattle is strong pure pastoralism is possible only in the tsetse-free areas.

This agriculture, even today, is mainly *subsistence* farming – production for use rather than sale of the staple food crops. It has been estimated that in all African countries outside the Republic of South Africa the majority of working Africans are still engaged in this traditional type of agriculture,[10] and that over the whole of tropical Africa between two thirds and three quarters of the total cultivated area is still used for subsistence production.[11]

Traditional agriculture is practised in most areas by the system

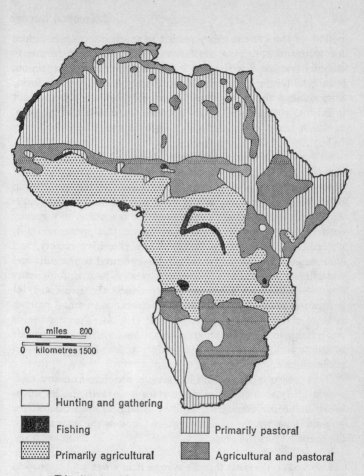

MAP 7. Distribution of types of subsistence economy. (Adapted from Murdock, G. P., *Africa, its Peoples and their Culture History*, 1959, p. 18)

known as *shifting cultivation* or *bush fallowing*. Under this system, each village has its own, perhaps ill-defined, tract of surrounding land. Working as a community the villagers will clear a section of their land, usually by cutting and burning of the scrub or woodland, and the land will then be cropped for several years until its fertility is exhausted. It is then allowed to lie fallow for

periods of from five to thirty years, and another section is cleared
for cultivation. During the fallow periods the land reverts to
scrubby woodland or 'bush' – even in the wetter areas it will not
usually be left long enough for the denser type of forest to form.
Surrounding the village itself there will be more permanent
individual plots, enriched by household rubbish and manure,
in which beans and fruits will be grown and where fowl may
be kept.

Shifting cultivation has been described as 'the greatest
obstacle not only to the immediate increase of agricultural
production, but also to the conservation of the production
potential of the future, in the form of soils and forests . . .'[12]
An intensification of agriculture and the transition to a money
economy is probably impossible under this system. It is,
nevertheless, not without its value in a primitive society, and
Worthington argues that it 'is admirably suited to the soils and
and climate of Africa, provided the area of land is sufficiently
large'.[13] Adequate fallowing does produce the necessary regeneration of the soil's fertility, and clearance in small patches
reduces the chances of excessive soil erosion. Trouble begins
when the pressure of population on the land reduces the periods
of fallow and as a consequence fertility and soil structure begin
to deteriorate.

This pressure on the land is a serious problem in many areas
and is likely to increase as death rates drop with the improvement in health standards. Dudley Stamp has calculated for
Nigeria how much land is required under the system. For
Southern Nigeria he says

I worked on the basis that the average family was 3.6 persons and
that each family required the produce from two acres of cultivation
annually. If the land is allowed to rest seven years after one year of
cultivation, each family would actually require sixteen acres of village
land. This gives a population density of 144 per square mile as the
maximum which can be supported . . . In Northern Nigeria, with a
lower and more precarious rainfall, I calculated . . . a density of
eighty-eight per square mile, above which the land would be over-
populated. There are indeed some parts of West Africa so crowded
that a year of cultivation is followed by only two years of bush
fallowing.[14]

Staple Food Crops

The staple crops grown in subsistence agriculture are those which give the maximum return of starchy food in a particular natural environment. Although the details vary,[15] tropical Africa can be divided into five main areas on the basis of the staple food types that are grown:

1. The forest areas west of the Bandama river in the Ivory Coast, where rice is the staple food crop. The area covers much of Guinea, Sierra Leone, and Liberia.

2. The other forest areas of west and central Africa, where various tropical roots – cassava (manioc), yams, taro (cocoyams), and sweet potatoes are dominant.

3. The drier, more northerly areas of the west, where cereals are of major importance, especially millets and sorghums, with some subsidiary maize, rice, groundnuts, and cow peas. Towards the southern edge of this region, in the relatively moist savanna areas, sweet potatoes are also grown.

4. The savanna country of the south and east, where maize is usually more important than millets and sorghums.

5. The Great Lakes area, where the plantain (green banana) forms the basis of the food supply.

Each crop tends to be dominant in the environment to which it is most suited and large areas of tropical Africa might remain uncultivated if any major group was missing. Millets and sorghums or maize are vital outside the forest areas; the tropical roots, plantains, or rice are vital within them – and yet only the millets and sorghums are native to Africa. The others have all been introduced into Africa since the beginning of the Christian era, and some are of much more recent date than that. Guinea yams east of the Ivory Coast and African rice to the west probably enabled man's conquest of the forest to begin, but these are not today's major staples in the forest areas.[16]

Thus, with the food plants native to Africa, the Negro cultivators could make effective penetration of none but the savanna country. Penetration of the equatorial and tropical rain forest, for which few suitable native plants were available, was only made easy with the introduction of the present food staples from outside the continent. It is not therefore surprising

TABLE 2

Major Tropical African Food Plants by Type and Origin

	Africa (South of Sahara)	S.E. Asia	America
Cereals	Millets & Sorghums African rice	Rice	Maize
Legumes	Cow pea		Haricot bean Lima bean
Tubers & Roots	Earth pea Guinea yam	Taro Yam	Cassava Ground nut Sweet potato
Fruits & Tree Crops	Oil palm Gourd Watermelon Tamarind	Plantain Banana Coconut Mango	Pineapple Pumpkin Squash Tomato Avocado Papaya
Condiments	Kola Coffee (Ethiopia)	Ginger Indian hemp	Cocoa Red pepper
Indulgents		Sugar cane Pepper Clove	Tobacco.

Crops which are dominant in the subsistence economy of particular areas are italicized.

SOURCE: Murdock, *Africa: its Peoples and their Culture History.*

that the earliest well organized African states were in the western Sudan* savanna country with millets and sorghums as the staple foods. The expansion of the Bantu into much of the southern and eastern parts of the continent did not take place until the arrival of exotic food plants from Asia.

These Asian food plants – yams, cocoyams and plantain in particular – were probably introduced to the east coast some time during and after the first century A.D., as this coast has had trading posts at least since then, posts established either by people of Indonesian origin, or Persians, or, since the seventh

*The term normally used for the northern part of west Africa, and not to be confused with the state of the same name which covers most of the eastern Sudan.

century, by Arabs.[17] The coastal traders were interested in the products of the interior, particularly slaves and ivory, and their expeditions into the hinterland were no doubt responsible for the initial westward diffusion of the Asian food plants. Once the Bantu had adopted them, they were able to displace the Pygmies and Bushmen from their former habitats and to reveal 'a capacity for explosive expansion paralleled, among all the other peoples of the world since the dawn of recorded history, only by the Arabs after Mohammed, the Chinese, and the European nations since the Discoveries . . .'[18]

Plants of American origin – notably maize and cassava – have clearly been introduced more recently, and were brought into West Africa by the Portuguese in the sixteenth century, to feed their slaves before and after shipment. Asian food plants may already by this time have reached the west coast from the east, enabling more effective colonization of the coastal forest zone from the inland empires.

The discovery of new foods does not necessarily presuppose the actual movement of large numbers of people at the same time. The knowledge may be passed on from village to village over the centuries until it has spread thousands of miles from its original source. Some such process has recently been outlined for the spread of cassava (manioc) in the Congo basin.

Late in the fifteenth century the Portuguese established relations with the King of the Congo at his capital some 200 miles inland from the mouth of the Congo, and for over a hundred years they maintained close relations with the Congolese. The rulers of the Kingdom of Congo apparently looked on the Europeans as representatives of a superior culture and were highly receptive to the innovations which they brought – so much so that by '1506 the King of Congo was the Christian ruler of a more or less Christian realm and recognized as such by the King of Portugal and by the Pope'. It would appear that at an early stage the Portuguese introduced manioc . . .[19]

Manioc, important in northern Angola as far back as the 1660s, had by 1885 been adopted by the Baluba Empire, a state covering most of what is now Katanga. It had taken just over 200 years for the knowledge of cassava cultivation to spread about 1,000 miles inland. If the Asian food plants from the east travelled at anything like this speed, they would have

reached the Guinea coast before the arrival there of the Portuguese.

The races of Africa and their ways of life before the modern
colonial period are thus fairly clearly discernible in broad
outline. Before the Christian era there were established Negro
civilizations in the west, Bushman and Pygmy hunters, together
with Caucasoid 'proto-Hamites' in the east, south, and centre
of the continent. Then, during the following centuries, came
the importation of alien food plants, bringing in their wake the
explosive expansion of the Bantu who, mixed with the earlier
stocks encountered, so creating greater racial complexity than
in the purely Negro west. The east African plateau from
Kenya southwards to the Republic of South Africa is relatively
open country, so that once the edge of the continent has been
breached, movement is comparatively easy. It is here that there
is the greatest tribal, linguistic, and racial complexity, quite
apart from the more recent introductions of Indian and European races and cultures. The term 'Bantu' alone covers great
racial and cultural complexities.[20]

In spite of the emphasis which many Africans themselves
place on cattle, their economies are – with a few exceptions –
based on agriculture, an agriculture which is mainly of the
traditional subsistence type and which is only now beginning to
change. Yet side by side with this subsistence economy there
exists today a completely different type of agricultural economy,
one which is commercial in motivation and usually modern in
technique. Often this commercial agriculture is run by Europeans and has certainly been introduced by them. The most
extreme contrasts are to be found in the Republic of South
Africa, with its highly successful European farming and the
still primitive agricultural methods of the poor and overcrowded African reserves. The marriage of these two contrasting
types of agricultural activity is one of Africa's important tasks
for the immediate future.

Notes on Chapter 2

1. Which divide the Mongoloid peoples of north and east Asia from the Caucasoids to the south.
2. See R. Oliver and J. D. Fage, *A Short History of Africa*, Chap. 1, Penguin African Library, 1962.
3. G. P. Murdock, *Africa, its Peoples and their Culture History*, 1959, p. 49. But see C. Turnbull, *The Forest People*, 1961, for an idealized view of Pygmy life by an anthropologist who has lived amongst them.
4. These paintings also have remarkable similarities to the much earlier efforts of stone age man in Europe.
   See L. Adam, *Primitive Art*, 1954.
5. Notably the Sandawe of N. Tanganyika and the Xhosa and Zulu of South Africa.
6. Height is a poor yardstick, except in extreme cases, as it is very much affected by diet.
7. J. H. Greenberg, *Studies in African Linguistic Classification*, 1955. Revised as *The Languages of Africa*, 1963, Mouton & Co., The Hague.
8. Oliver and Fage, op. cit., p. 29.
9. W. O. Jones, *Manioc in Africa* – quoted in Johnston, *The Staple Food Economies of Western Tropical Africa*, 1958, p. 177.
10. U.N. Dept. of Econ. & Soc. Affairs. *Economic Survey of Africa since* 1950.
11. op. cit., p. 99.
12. F.A.O. Staff, 'Shifting Cultivation' in *Tropical Agriculture*, July 1957, quoted in Johnston, op. cit., 266.
13. op. cit., p. 11.
14. L. D. Stamp. 'Land Utilization and Soil Erosion in Nigeria', in *Geographical Review*, 1938, pp. 32–45 and quoted in Stamp, op. cit., p. 151.

15. SOME CHARACTERISTICS OF THE MAJOR CROPS.

Millets and Sorghums need less water than any other cereals, and are unique in being able to stand periods of drought, after which they recover to recommence growth normally. They are also resistant to hot dry air, a fact of special importance in the west, with its periodic 'Harmattan' winds blowing off the Sahara. They are tolerant in their soil requirements and have a fairly short growing season. Low yields are the rule in the difficult conditions under which they are usually grown, but they have proved particularly suitable to savanna country.

Rice in the west is usually upland rice, which does not need flooded paddy fields for its cultivation. Swamp rice with its much higher yields but also more complicated techniques of cultivation has only been grown on a large scale in recent years, and in commercial as distinct from subsistence farming.

Maize needs more water than millets and sorghums, although it is partially drought-resistant, except at the 'tasselling' stage. It does not like dry heat, which probably explains why it is less important in the west than in the east and south. Its great advantage is that cultivation is much easier than for millets and sorghums, while the yields are higher in suitable conditions. On the other hand, owing to the wider spacing between the plants, it does encourage soil erosion.

Plantains need fairly rich soils, good drainage and an ample, well-distributed rainfall. In such favourable areas very high yields are possible. These areas occur on the volcanic soils of the Great Lakes region and in Cameroon.

Cassava (Manioc) is the most versatile of the tropical roots. Even on poor soils it will give high yields, a fact which probably explains its increased use on some of the exhausted soils of Nigeria. It gives a certain yield even in soils unsuitable for all other crops and is very easy to cultivate.

Yams occur in several varieties, some of which can survive under drier conditions than cassava.

Taro (Cocoyams) have similar requirements to cassava, but can survive on less well-drained soils and in shade. With their large leaves they are often planted as a crop to protect young cocoa trees from the sun.

Sweet Potatoes need less moisture than the other tropical roots and will mature in 3–4 months.

For more details on crops see F. R. Irvine, *A Textbook of West African Agriculture, Soils and Crops*, 1953

16. See J. D. Fage, 'Anthropology, Botany and the History of Africa', *Journal of African History*, 1961, II, 2, p. 299.

17. The Portuguese were also active along the east coast from the sixteenth century.

18. Murdock, op. cit., p. 271.

19. Johnston, op. cit., p. 177, quoting W. O. Jones.

20. But see Noni Jabavu, *Drawn in Colour*, 1960, for a vivid comparison of two Bantu societies.

3 Europe Goes into Africa

EARLY CONTACTS

The period of colonial rule in Africa has been relatively short. For over 400 years the coastline had been known and increasingly dominated by the European powers, but the interior remained unknown and unwanted until the end of the nineteenth century. This was not only because of the inhospitable coasts and the difficulty of penetrating beyond them, but also because what was considered useful to Europeans could be had without bothering to penetrate far inland. Small coastal forts were all that were required to provide bases for ships on their way to the known riches of the East and to act as depots for the plunder of the interior. Gold, ivory, and, above all, slaves could be brought to the European forts by native middlemen.

The Portuguese were the earliest coastal explorers and the first of Africa's European colonists. Creeping southwards along the west coast, the ships of Prince Henry the Navigator had already reached south of the Gambia by the time of his death in 1460, and they had brought back with them their first cargoes of gold and slaves. By 1484, Diego Cão had reached the mouth of the Congo, and before the century was out Vasco da Gama's discovery of the Cape route to India made possible the rapid expansion of a Portuguese empire in the Indian Ocean.

North of Cape Delgado, on the east coast, the Portuguese found the Arabs already entrenched. From their coastal bases the Arabs were able to obtain precisely the same African commodities that interested the Portuguese; like them, they failed to penetrate into the interior until well into the nineteenth century.

The Portuguese monopoly of west Africa and of the slave trade lasted until the end of the sixteenth century, when it was broken by a number of west European countries. French, English, Danes, and Prussians all established rival forts and entered the trade, but it was the Dutch who really ousted the Portuguese from their dominating position, both in west Africa and in the Indian Ocean. In the west the Portuguese were driven from all their strongholds except on the coast of what is now Portuguese Guinea and Angola. In the east they were similarly driven southwards by the Arabs to what is now Moçambique.

The slave trade reached its height in the eighteenth century, and the Dutch and English were the chief carriers. Various estimates of the number taken out of Africa have been made, but it was certainly not less than ten million and may well have been more. One careful calculation gives twelve million for the Atlantic trade alone, while the Arab trade in the east probably involved even greater numbers,[1] covering as it did a much longer period of time.* What has horrified subsequent generations produced no moral qualm among those involved, and it took thirty-one years from the date of the first unsuccessful motion against the slave trade in the British House of Commons to the final abolition of slavery for Britain itself in 1807. The long period for which the trade flourished has been called

an appalling illustration of the strength which vested interests can acquire, and of the extent to which familiarity with crime can deaden the conscience and blur discrimination between plain right and wrong. The first British African Company was formed for honest trade, and ships sent to the Gambia refused to buy negro women offered for sale by a negro on the ground that Englishmen did not buy and sell 'any that had our own shapes'. . . but slave trading became the main-stay of West African commerce. Thenceforward there was no question as to the morality of the traffic; the great issue was whether it should be monopolized by a company or thrown open to competition. . . . Slave labour had become a matter of course . . .[2]

The slave trade was, however, more than a crime against humanity and a challenge to the conscience of Europe. Many of its effects were to endure much longer than the trade itself, influencing the life of Africa today as an inevitable legacy from the past. Of these effects, there are three of outstanding im-portance.

*It started before the Christian era.

Firstly, there are the effects arising from the forcible mass movement of millions of Negroes to the Americas, where they have increased in numbers and extended their range of distribution since the days of slavery. They have become integrated in varying degrees with the societies in which they now live, but, because of the consciousness of colour that those with lighter skins have forced upon them, they have never completely lost their sense of identity with their African origins. For some, like those who supported Marcus Garvey in the 1920s, this sense has implied an eventual return to Africa; for others it has meant participating in African emancipation from the outside by encouraging the 'Pan-Africanist' movement; while for the majority it has entailed a simple emotional affinity with all other Negroes. In all instances, their sense of identity has given them a heightened interest in the welfare of Africa – an interest which the political leaders of countries like the U.S.A. and the West Indies can afford to ignore only at their peril.

Secondly, the slave trade perpetuated the isolation of the interior long after normal trade and empire building would have opened it up. The interior of Africa became the preserve of the slave traders and their agents, a locked-up land in which there was neither room nor opportunity for the teacher, scientist, or missionary. The slavers could obtain all they wanted from their bases on the coast. It was in their interests, as Livingstone saw so clearly, to keep Africa an 'unknown' continent, just as the only way to kill the slave trade was to open up the interior and provide both facilities and security for honest trade.[3]

Thirdly, slave trading helped to destroy the native civilizations of the interior. It did so in two ways: by maintaining a state of perpetual inter-tribal warfare, as tribe raided tribe to secure captives to sell to the slavers, and by the depopulation of whole areas over a long period of time. It thus helped to reinforce the European belief that nothing good could come out of Africa except what was put into it by Europeans. It helped to perpetuate the myth that the Negro was inherently inferior, so that as late as 1928 a distinguished Englishman could write:

The Negroes of Tropical Africa specialized in their isolation and stagnated in utter savagery. They may even have been drifting away from the human standard back towards the brute when migratory impulses drew the Caucasian, the world's redeemer, to enter Tropical Africa . . . mingle his blood with that of the pristine negroes and raise the mental status of these dark skinned, woolly haired, prognathous retrograded men . . .[4]

Echoes of this attitude were still to be heard in the British House of Lords in 1961:

As I went to it [the United Nations] I really got the impression that there was a convention of nigger minstrels going on . . . the Commonwealth is a piebald set-up, and a piebald set-up is a poor form of organization that will never last.[5]

The one exception to the general European lack of interest in the interior was that of the Dutch in South Africa. The first settlement was planted in 1652, when Jan Van Riebeeck was commissioned to build a fort and re-victualling station at the Cape of Good Hope for ships of the Dutch East India Company. Although the Company did not intend to establish a colony, it soon realized that the most economical way of obtaining fresh food was to import Europeans to farm the land. In 1687 a policy of active colonization was initiated, and by 1706 the colony consisted of 1,641 people, who by this time had spread far out into the hinterland in search of more land and freedom from the restrictions of authority. By 1779 the settlers had their first clash with westward-moving Bantu tribes in the region of the present Ciskei reserve.*

To the Afrikaner, ever since, the black African has remained the enemy on the other side of the frontier, however absurd this has geographically become.

Apart from the movement inland of the Cape Dutch, Africa remained an unknown land to Europeans until the great explorations of the nineteenth century: explorations which were to draw the main outlines of the interior and to provide that foundation of geographical knowledge on which the political partition of the continent was to be based.

EUROPE TAKES OVER

The earliest explorations and the earliest political divisions took place in the west. Under the auspices of the African Association

*See Chapter 12 below.

of London, Mungo Park visited the Gambia river in 1795 and made his way overland to the river Niger. Prior to this journey it was believed that the Gambia and Senegal rivers were the outlets for a westward-flowing Niger. He returned to the Niger ten

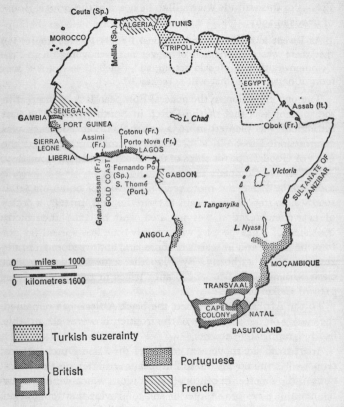

MAP 8. The pattern of alien rule, 1880. (From J. D. Fage, *An Atlas of African History*, 1958, p. 46)

years later with the intention of following its course to the sea, but he was unsuccessful and died believing that the Niger and the Congo shared the same estuary. It was not until the 1830 journey of the Lander brothers that the outlet of the Niger was finally discovered.

Political involvement in west Africa by the European powers remained very small until the last two decades of the nineteenth century. Intervention in the hinterland at this time was usually reluctant and designed for the protection of the trading, missionary, and humanitarian interests already established there.

The British navy had been the chief instrument in the suppression of the slave trade, and to this end bases had been acquired* in order to drive out the slavers, encourage legitimate commerce, and facilitate the advance of 'civilization'. There was, however, little desire to acquire an empire.

One of the unforeseen consequences of this peaceful European intrusion into the affairs of west Africa was a further breakdown of tribal authority, especially on the coast, and a consequent increase in unrest and warfare. In the Gold Coast, for example, Britain was drawn into wars with the Ashanti in 1863 and 1864 – wars which brought trade to a standstill. Such seemed the hopelessness of the situation that a Select Committee of the House of Commons was led to recommend a withdrawal from all existing bases in west Africa apart from Sierra Leone.[6]

A withdrawal of this nature was easier to recommend than to achieve. However reluctant the original involvement may have been, Britain's commitments tended rather to increase. Far from withdrawing from the Gold Coast, a further Ashanti attack in 1873, threatening as it did the existing British bases, led to an extension of British influence over the coastal Fanti and, in 1874, to the establishment of the Gold Coast as a Crown Colony. Even if it had wanted to, Britain dared not give up its west African responsibilities for fear of offending humanitarian opinion.[7]

The French, too, were reluctant to engage in colonial expansion at this time. Except for the colonial government in Senegal, they were content to have the same sort of indirect influence through missionaries and traders that Britain sought to exercise. In Senegal, which appears to have developed 'a local expansive power of its own',[8] the urge to empire took hold early, and the advance inland to the upper Niger began in 1876. When the French government finally did take an interest in a west African empire (after 1882), the systematic eastward penetration from

*Sierra Leone in 1808, Gambia in 1816 and Gold Coast in 1821.

Senegal over the previous few years gave them an important advantage over their rivals.

The west had been explored, but the whole of the central and eastern parts of the continent remained unknown when David Livingstone started on his first journey in 1841. Moving northwards from the Cape of Good Hope he discovered Lake Ngami in Bechuanaland eight years later, mapped out the upper Zambezi in the following year, and arrived at Luanda on the coast of Angola in 1854. In another two years he had made the first coast-to-coast crossing of the continent, discovered the Victoria Falls, and mapped out the whole of the Zambezi river. Previously an agent of the London Missionary Society, he embarked on his second journey in 1858 as a government servant with consular authority, exploring during six more years the Shiré river and the Shiré highlands of Nyasaland (now Malawi).

Meanwhile, farther north, Burton and Speke moving west from Zanzibar had discovered Lake Tanganyika in 1858. Their journey, together with the later ventures of Speke and Grant and those of Sir Samuel Baker, had at last found the source of the Nile by the time Livingstone returned in 1864. It still remained to determine the source of the Congo and whether or not Lake Tanganyika was linked with the Nile.

Livingstone started on his final journey in 1866, exploring in what is now Zambia. He died on the shores of Lake Tanganyika in 1871, and it was left to Stanley to solve the final river problem of Africa. In 1877 he succeeded in passing down the Lualaba and Congo rivers to the sea. The main physical features of the continent were now known to Europe and the stage was set for the 'scramble' by the European powers for pieces of African territory, a scramble which in less than twenty years was to transform the political map and trace today's international boundaries.

'The Scramble for Africa' rates an important place in most history books of the period, but much less is known about it than is popularly supposed. Up to the 1880s none of the European powers had shown much interest in taking on more responsibilities in tropical Africa. They had been content to protect the interests of private citizens already established there while holding back from more formal commitments to empire-building.

Now the political map of Africa was to be re-drawn and almost
the whole of the continent placed under European rule. What
was it that set off this partition?

The motives of statesmen were certainly mixed, and the
Leninist 'search for markets'[9] is rather too simple an explanation to be more than part of the truth. In fact there was never
enough investment in tropical Africa to provide for the creation
there of the vast consumer markets which may be expected to
arise in the future. This does not imply that a search for markets
was not one of the motives behind the scramble, but there was
much more to it than that. Raw material needs in Europe were
also important, and so were philanthropy, missionary endeavour,
strategic pressures – like the protection of Britain's sea-route to
India – and the search for political prestige *in Europe itself*.

Europe was ruled by a 'balance of power', in which one of the
major tests of prestige and influence was the loss or gain of
territory. What had happened in the past to Poland and more
recently to Alsace was now to occur in Africa. European diplo-
mats began to use stretches of African soil, known to them only
as coloured areas on inaccurate maps, as bargaining counters in
the struggle for power in Europe.[10]

A recent careful analysis of cabinet and other government
papers[11] has shown that – for Britain at least – the overriding
motive in acquiring a new empire in Africa was a concern for the
security of the routes to the old empire in India. This meant a
keen interest in the east coast, where there were thought to be
few opportunities for trade, and much less interest in the west,
where the chief commercial opportunities were known to be. It
meant, above all, that stability in Egypt was the first priority in
Africa for Britain's late Victorian statesmen.

The British occupation of Egypt in 1882 was undertaken to
protect the Suez Canal and to prevent its control by a hostile
government. It was not meant to be the start of a scramble for
territory elsewhere in the continent, but this it turned out to be.
The occupation of Egypt alienated France from Britain and
gave Germany an opportunity to exploit their differences to her
own advantage.

By altering the European balance the occupation of Egypt inflated
the importance of trivial disputes in tropical Africa and set off a

scramble. Quickened by the hope of prising the British out of Cairo, the French drove deep into West Africa, while the Germans took their opportunity to irrupt into East and West Africa, in an attempt to extort British support in Europe. Hence the taking of Egypt ended the age when private merchants and consuls, acting through African authorities, could dominate the east and west coasts by influence alone. Once the French and German governments for diplomatic purposes began to back their own traders against British firms, trade turned into a business of territorial claims.[12]

There were plenty of traders and adventurers already active in Africa to whom the European governments could now turn to help them in their own power struggles. One of these was Stanley who, in 1878, returned to the Congo under the auspices of the newly formed International Association of the Congo, a body international only in name and in reality under the control of its President, Leopold, King of the Belgians, acting in his personal capacity.

Both France and Portugal were also active at the mouth of the Congo, and the Association soon found itself in dispute with these countries over territorial claims. To settle the disputes between these rivals, Bismarck of Germany called the Berlin Africa Conference of 1884–5.

The Conference produced the Berlin Act, an instrument signed by all the major European powers. It aimed 'to foster the development of trade and civilization, to further the moral and material well-being of the native populations', and to abolish slavery in the area. It provided for the establishment of a free trade area and for the neutralization of the whole of central Africa in the event of a European war. It also attempted to regulate the process of further territorial acquisitions by the powers.

Immediately following the Berlin Conference the area allotted to the International Association was organized as the 'Congo Free State' with Leopold as King – again in his personal capacity. It became a classic example of misrule and exploitation. Leopold seems to have run a kind of rake's progress through the Congo. Concessions were given to companies which went into partnership with the government. The native population was deprived of its land, driven to forced labour and treated with horrible cruelty.[13] The atrocity charges were fully authenticated and led the British Foreign Secretary to declare that the state had 'morally forfeited every right to international recognition.'[14] The worst features of misrule ceased after Leopold's death, and the State was taken over as a Belgian Colony in 1908.

The rest of the partition tale is best told on the accompanying maps and was virtually completed in the ten years following on the Berlin Conference. In the east, British and Italian Somaliland, Uganda, Kenya, and German East Africa all appeared. In the west, the essentials of present-day boundaries were established while, in the south, Rhodes's advance northwards with his British South Africa Company had frustrated the claims of Portugal to all the lands between Angola and Moçambique. German-British affairs in Africa were settled by the Anglo-German Treaty of 1890 which, among other provisions, exchanged Heligoland for British control over Zanzibar.

THE DRAWING OF FRONTIERS

The newly independent African states are no more free of the frontiers of the 'scramble' than they were in their colonial past. Some, like Ghana, Guinea, and Mali, have made attempts to escape from the old boundaries. Others, like Tanganyika, express their intention to do so.* Only British and Italian Somaliland, the Republic of Cameroun, and the Southern Cameroons have so far united in practice across colonial frontiers. And this is not surprising, for the administrations and other vested interests which have developed within the artificially created boundaries are no less strong than tribal and economic interests which pull across them.

Not only was the partition undertaken solely in the interests of Europe, but the advance into the hinterland was inevitably made from existing bases on the coast. Thus in West Africa most of the colonies came to have a north-south orientation quite at variance with the human and physical divisions, which run east-west. Again, in the Rhodesias the advance had to take place from the existing Cape Colony, avoiding the Portuguese-held

*And has now succeeded in forming, in 1964, the United Republic of Tanzania.

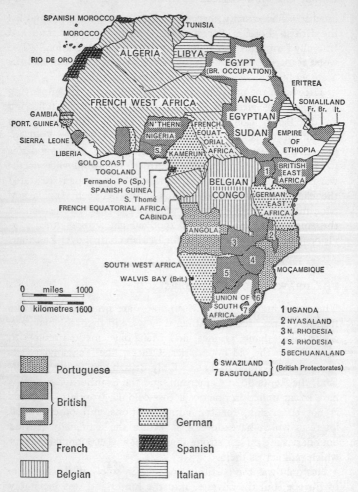

MAP 9. The pattern of alien rule, 1914. (From J. D. Fage, *An Atlas of African History*, 1958, p. 48)

coasts and the Boer Republics, and moving across the most open type of terrain.

British colonization was conducted either by chartered companies, as in Southern Rhodesia, or by officials who took the

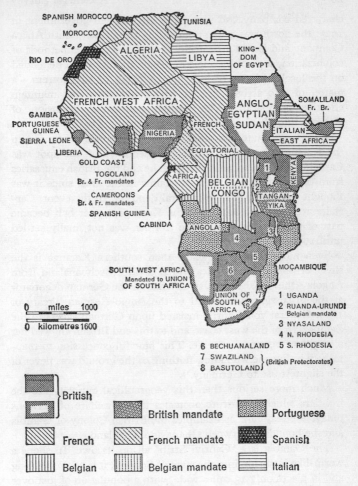

MAP 10. The pattern of alien rule, 1939. (From J. D. Fage, *An Atlas of African History*, 1958, p. 49)

existing native authorities under their protection, as in Northern Rhodesia and Uganda. The two methods of taking control have had profoundly different effects on subsequent development. In the Rhodesias, for example, the south was conquered by a

chartered company and was given internal self-government in
1923: the north was not conquered by the British South Africa
Company and is still a Protectorate.* Whatever the methods of
colonization, control by one country or another often depended
on the local initiative of individual officials or adventurers – a
matter of who arrived first or who could prove and maintain
effective occupation. The curious southward extension of
Katanga into Northern Rhodesia was promoted in this way.

The Congo State had already given a minerals concession to
the Katanga Company, whose representative on the spot was
Captain Carstairs, a Canadian. Both he and the British emissaries
from the south wished to stake claims in the area, since it was
thought to be very rich in mineral deposits. In the event, Carstairs arrived first (1891) and the Katanga copper belt became
part of the Congo; though the frontier was not finally settled
until 1930.

Even more curious in shape than southern Katanga is the
sliver of South West Africa which divides Bechuanaland from
Angola – the Caprivi strip, so called after the German negotiator
at the discussions which led to the Anglo-German Treaty of
1890. General von Caprivi insisted upon German access to the
Zambezi from the west coast, and to this end Britain allowed her
a corridor twenty miles wide. This fanciful concession to map-
makers in Europe who knew nothing of the ground was never of
the slightest use to Germany.[15]

Much more serious than this geographical curiosity are the
frontiers which constitute obstacles to the welfare of Africans
today. We may take as examples the British Colony of Gambia
and the boundary between Ghana and Togoland.

The Gambia is a 'Caprivi Strip' all on its own. In shape a
worm-like intrusion into the state of Senegal, it is 300 miles long
and in places only 13 miles wide, with a population of just over
a quarter of a million. It lies astride the navigable section of the
Gambia river, which is itself one of the finest stretches of navigable water in the whole of Africa. Ocean-going ships can reach

* It became, in October 1964, the independent state of Zambia, while the immediate future of the south is still uncertain at the time of writing.

150 miles up river from Bathurst, and but for the existence of political boundaries the Gambia would undoubtedly be the main outlet for the trade of both Senegal and Mali.

British control of the Gambia meant that the French had to make alternative transport arrangements, and the Gambia has been used only for local traffic. As the Senegal river is much less navigable, the main line of communication has been the railway from Kayes to Dakar, built in 1923, a costly undertaking which also required the costly construction of a large artificial harbour at Dakar. This would all have been unnecessary if the more convenient Bathurst could have been utilized.

Not only has the separation of Gambia from its hinterland led to the wasteful construction of railway and port facilities in Senegal and the neglect of the Gambia itself, but the development of part of Senegal has also been retarded. Gambia Colony separated the southern province of Casamance from the rest of the country, and because of the difficulties of communication economic development there has been slow. Only in 1947 did Britain agree to give the French direct transport facilities between the two parts of Senegal.

The Ghana-Togoland boundary divides the Ewe people into two more or less equal parts. Numbering about one million in all, about half now live in south-east Ghana and the rest in southern Togoland. Prior to independence repeated representations about their division were made by Ewe leaders, both at the League of Nations and at the U.N.* The Ewe tended until recently to prefer British to French rule, and there was at one time some movement of population from the French to the English side of the frontier. Their agitation for unity received support from nationalist leaders in the Gold Coast, but since the independence of Togo the Ewe there have shown no significant interest in joining independent Ghana.

Whatever the difficulties that the existing frontiers create, it is clear that they will be slow to change now independence has been achieved. The establishment of an independent government creates a vested interest in the perpetuation of the existing

* Most of the territory involved was under League mandate or, later, U.N. Trusteeship.

political unit – or at any rate in the prevention of its absorption by its neighbour.

As has been seen, Europe surrounded and exploited Africa long before the interior was seized or even explored. When the interior was finally opened up, it was from a mixture of motives – some benevolent and some selfish – but all of them assumed the supremacy of Europe and the benefits which would result from European rule.

This is not the place to draw up a balance sheet on colonialism, but it has been shown that the hurried and largely haphazard nature of the scramble for Africa did little good from the outset to some of the areas involved. Lasting frontiers were established which cut across both ethnic and economic interests, and which to many of those drawing them were simply lines on inadequate and little understood maps.

Subsequent developments have brought remarkable changes during the last sixty years. The Eurocentric view of Africa has gradually given way to a recognition that the continent matters for itself and that the interests of the inhabitants should ultimately determine policy. It remains true, however, that even the most revolutionary changes have up to now taken place within the geographical framework, the main political outlines of which were established during the scramble at the end of the nineteenth century.

Notes on Chapter 3

1. R. Coupland, *East Africa and its Invaders*, 1938, p. 35.
2. C. P. Lucas, *The Partition of Africa*, 1922, pp. 50–51 and Coupland, op. cit., Chapter 1.
3. Lucas, op. cit., p. 53.
4. Sir H. H. Johnston, *The Opening Up of Africa*, 1928, p. 25.
5. Lord Brabazon of Tara, 23 March 1961, *Hansard*, Vol. 229, No. 57, Cols. 1277–9.
6. R. Robinson, J. Gallagher, and A. Denny, *Africa and the Victorians*, 1961, p. 30.
7. ibid., p. 33.
8. ibid., p. 163.
9. See J. A. Hobson, *Imperialism*, 1902, and V. I. Lenin, *Imperialism, the Highest Stage of Capitalism*, 1916.
10. C. E. Carrington, 'Frontiers in Africa'. In *International Affairs*, Vol. 36, No. 4, October 1960, p. 431.
11. Robinson, Gallagher, and Denny, op. cit.
12. ibid., p. 162.
13. Lucas, op. cit., p. 85.
14. Sir Ed. Grey, quoted ibid., p. 85.
15. For a more detailed treatment of these and other frontier problems see R. J. Harrison Church, *Modern Colonization*, 1951, Chap. 7.
    See also Nordholt, *The People that Walk in Darkness*, 1960.

4 Natural Resources and Economic Development

The improvement of living standards and the elimination of poverty are aims which are shared by all the countries of Africa whatever their political complexion. The belief in the possibility of achieving these aims is, however, something new, and the will to do something about it is even newer. It is easy to forget that most African governments only began comprehensive economic development with the end of the Second World War. As a result there is a tremendous amount of knowledge still to be gained about the continent's natural wealth, and it is impossible to say with any certainty how rich in resources Africa will prove to be.

Outside South Africa, the economic potential of the continent remains largely unexplored and underdeveloped, with only isolated pockets here and there of intensive economic activity, both in agriculture and industry. Apart from South Africa and, to a lesser extent, Kenya and Southern Rhodesia, there is little manufacturing industry, and most of the economic development has been concentrated on those crops (like cocoa in Ghana) or minerals (like copper in Northern Rhodesia) unobtainable in Europe or obtainable more cheaply in Africa. In each instance the markets lie outside Africa, and development has been undertaken in response to an overseas demand. Another type of development has taken place where favourable climates have attracted European settlers (as in Kenya and Southern Rhodesia). Because of their European contacts these settlers have succeeded in attracting a disproportionate amount of investment capital, a fact which has helped to maintain the uneven character of development in the continent as a whole.

African poverty is real enough. Even allowing for considerable margins of error, the figures in Table 3 show an average so low that it is difficult for the West European or North American to imagine it.

TABLE 3

National Income per Head in Selected Countries (1961 estimates in dollars)

United Kingdom	1163
Republic of South Africa	376
Ghana	244
Kenya	74
Uganda	65
Tanganyika	57

SOURCE: *U.N. Statistical Year Book 1962*, pp. 21–36 and 487–8.

POPULATION

The people of any country are important economically both as consumers and as producers. Fears of over-population, which have in recent years led to a greater emphasis on their role as consumers, should not make us forget that as producers people are the first essential economic resource which any country must have. There are about 190 million people in tropical and southern Africa, and although in a few areas population density is high, the continent as a whole is still very sparsely inhabited; for the most part, the density falls below fifty persons to the square mile. (Map No. 11.) This low density is certainly a reflection of the real present poverty, whatever may be the potential wealth in terms of population and production.

The patches of denser than average population seem to be connected with development beyond a purely subsistence economy. Those based on industry are all in South Africa, notably on the Witwatersrand and near Cape Town, Port Elizabeth, and Durban.[1] The other higher densities shown on the map are almost entirely agricultural.

In the east there are five main areas: the coast from Mombasa to Dar-es-Salaam, the Lake Victoria region, the highland areas of Kenya and of Tanganyika, and south Malawi. Although these areas differ greatly in their climates, soils, crops, racial complexity, and social systems, they have all moved beyond a system of subsistence agriculture, and in each of them a considerable proportion of effort is devoted to producing crops for sale. Similarly in the west the two discontinuous belts of higher density are based partly on cash crops – groundnuts and market gardening in the northern areas, and palm oil and cocoa in the southern. If the map were on a larger scale, mining areas like the Rhodesian and Katangan copper belts would also appear as small areas of higher density.[2]

TABLE 4

Population (1961 Estimates)

	Population (in 1000s)	Area (in sq. Kms)	Density (per sq. Kms.)
West Africa (English-speaking)			
Nigeria (1964)	55,653	878,447	64
Ghana	6,943	237,873	29
Sierra Leone	2,450	72,326	34
Gambia	267	10,369	26
Liberia (1960)	1,290	111,370	12
West Africa (French-speaking)			
Cameroun (1960)	4,097	432,500	9
Guinea (1960)	3,000	245,857	12
Mali (1960)	4,100	1,204,021	3
Niger (1960)	2,870	1,188,794	2
Dahomey	2,050	115,762	18
Upper Volta (1960)	3,635	274,122	13
Ivory Coast	3,300	322,463	10
Senegal	2,980	197,161	15
Mauretania (1960)	727	1,085,805	1
Togo	1,480	57,000	26
Former French Equatorial Africa			
Chad	2,680	1,284,000	2
Central African Republic	1,227	617,000	2
Gabon (1960)	440	267,000	2
Congo (ex-French) (1960)	795	342,000	2
East Africa			
Kenya (1962 census)	8,676	582,646	15
Uganda	6,845	243,410	29
Tanganyika	9,399	937,061	10
Zanzibar and Pemba	315	2,643	119
Ruanda and Burundi (1960)	4,901	54,172	90
Former Belgian Congo	14,464	2,344,932	6

	Population (in 1000s)	Area (in sq. Kms)	Density (per sq. Kms.)
Spanish and Portuguese Territories			
Angola	4,870	1,246,700	4
Moçambique	6,650	783,030	8
São Tomé & Principe	64	964	66
Portuguese Guinea (1960)	571	36,125	16
Fernando Po and Annobon (1960)	63	3,034	31
Rio Muni	185	—	7
Central Africa Commonwealth			
Zambia	2,480	746,256	3
Rhodesia	3,150	389,362	9
Malawi	2,890	117,498	24
Southern Africa			
Republic of South Africa	16,236	1,223,409	13
S.W. Africa	534	823,876	1
Basutoland	697	730,342	23
Bechuanaland	332	712,249	1
Swaziland	266	17,363	15
Total Population: 183,572			

Areas of Some Non-African Countries for Comparison (in sq. km's)

U.S.	9,363,387
India	3,263,373
France	551,208
Belgium	30,507
U.K.	244,016
England & Wales	151,113

SOURCE: *U.N. Statistical Year Book 1961*, pp. 21–6,
U.N. Statistical Year Book 1962, pp. 21–5.

The economic development of Africa has been even more patchy and haphazard than the population distribution indicates; there are great contrasts in the rate of economic growth from territory to territory and even within individual countries. Existing economic activity is carried on in a series of economic 'islands', often separated by great spaces devoted almost entirely to subsistence agriculture. These islands can usually be classified under three headings: the coastal areas, where access to overseas

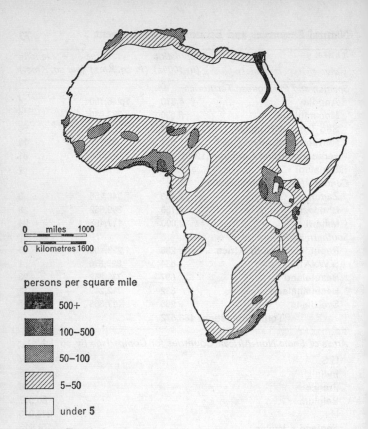

persons per square mile

- 500+
- 100–500
- 50–100
- 5–50
- under 5

MAP 11. Population density

markets is easy and of long standing; the highland areas, where superior climates and soils have attracted European farmers; and the mining centres. 'These distinct and separate economic islands combined make up perhaps 4 per cent of the area of tropical Africa, but probably account for at least 85 per cent of the value of produce entering world trade.'[3]

Another way of comparing present incomes is to examine the export figures, for African countries live by the export of food and raw materials in so far as their inhabitants are engaged in the money economy at all.

TABLE 5

Value of Exports and Imports 1951

Country	(Millions of U.S. Dollars) Imports	Exports	(U.S. Dollars) Exports per head of population
São Tome and Principe	5	8	133
Rhodesias and Nyasaland	420	523	65
Liberia	43	65	52
Ghana	317	286	44
Zanzibar and Pemba	15	13	43
Cameroun	82	108	36
Congo (ex-Belgian) (including Ruanda and Burundi)	308	489	35
Gambia	9	8	27
Angola	131	124	27
Sierra Leone	66	54	22
Former French Equatorial Africa	127	90	18
Togo	15	18	18
Kenya, Uganda, and Tanganyika	340	357	16
Former French West Africa (excluding Guinea)	309	269	15
Nigeria	502	458	14
Moçambique	122	73	12
Portuguese Guinea	8	7	12

SOURCE: *U.N. Statistical Year Book 1960*, p. 390.

Partly for reasons of prestige and partly from sound economic motives African countries would like to reduce their dependence on the export of primary products. Industry is necessary both to satisfy national pride and for economic well-being. If a country relies solely on the export of primary products it is inevitably at the mercy of economic conditions in the advanced industrial countries. A slight fall in industrial production in Europe, for example, can lead to a catastrophic fall in the export income of an underdeveloped country. Nevertheless, the development of manufacturing industry is likely to be a slow process.

Private capital is always more readily available for the expansion of mining, and public investment will have to continue to concern itself above all with improving basic services like transport and power supplies. It follows, therefore, that the export of primary products either from the land or from the mines will provide the main source of revenue for some time to come.

AGRICULTURE – THE PRESENT POSITION

The land devoted to producing crops for sale – both in the internal and external markets – varies from one quarter to one third of the total cultivated area of tropical Africa, but even where the proportion of cash-crop production is high, it is all too often concentrated on one or two crops of high profitability. Not enough has been done to develop other lines as an insurance against a fall in prices. Dependence on groundnuts in Senegal and Gambia and cocoa in Ghana means prosperity while prices are high but may lead to disaster with a fall in overseas demand. This dependence on one or two crops is probably inevitable as long as development is left uncoordinated and uncontrolled, because such crops are immediately profitable, while those increases in production which have occurred in recent years have followed the classic African pattern in being largely haphazard and in response to overseas demand.

Coffee production in 1959 was over twice the level of that in 1950, with expansion particularly rapid in former French West Africa, Cameroun, Congo (ex-Belgian), and East Africa. Tea production, especially in Kenya and Tanganyika, has also more than doubled in a decade. Sisal in Tanganyika is more than 50 per cent above the 1950 level, and there have been even more spectacular increases in rubber production, with a fourfold increase in the Congo (ex-Belgian) and a fivefold increase in Nigeria.[4]

These increases are impressive and economically important to the countries concerned, but all of them are for crops which are either luxuries or industrial raw materials, and there has been much less effort and investment put into the production of food, which is still largely the function of subsistence agriculture. However, the success of the export crops lends support to the view that the islands of commercial farming could be extended and that 'there is sound reason for the belief that trans-Saharan Africa could become much more productive agriculturally than hitherto'.[5]

MINING AND POWER SUPPLIES

It is clear that Africa is rich in both minerals and power supplies, although there is much exploratory work still to be done. The deficiency in coal and oil[6] is offset by a large hydro-electric potential – about 40 per cent of the world total – and for a large number of minerals Africa is already a leading producer. With few exceptions, production has increased rapidly since pre-war days, in some cases spectacularly so. Between 1950 and 1959 copper rose by 75 per cent, manganese by 48 per cent, chrome by 86 per cent, and bauxite – a late starter – by 348 per cent.

TABLE 6

Production of Principal Minerals

1948–50 average = 100

Minerals	Level of Production 1937–38 average	Level of Production 1957–59 average
Copper	91	175
Manganese	68	148
Iron	96	194
Lead	56	206
Zinc	31	239
Tin	91	92
Bauxite	—	348
Chromite	54	186
Cobalt	55	202
Gold	132	137

SOURCES: *U.N. Economic Survey of Africa since 1950*, p. 115, *U.N. Statistical Year Book 1960*

As with any generalizations made on a continental scale, the figures in Table 7 conceal not only differing growth rates for different countries, but also the fact that only a minority of countries are important mineral producers. Out of a total of thirty-six countries in tropical and southern Africa, only eight are major producers of any mineral, with another five as significant minor producers. (See Map No. 12.)[7]

By value, 42.6 per cent of the total mineral output is in South Africa, 17.6 per cent in the Rhodesias, and 15.9 per cent in the

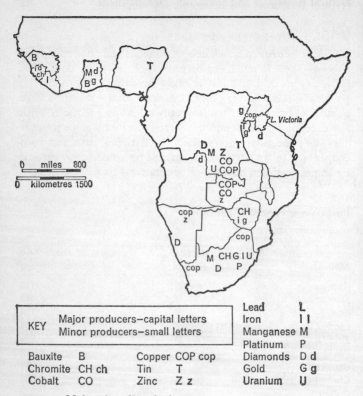

KEY — Major producers—capital letters
Minor producers—small letters

				Lead	L	
				Iron	l I	
				Manganese	M	
				Platinum	P	
Bauxite	B	Copper	COP cop	Diamonds	D d	
Chromite	CH ch	Tin	T	Gold	G g	
Cobalt	CO	Zinc	Z z	Uranium	U	

MAP 12. Main mineral producing areas

Congo (ex-Belgian), and it is these countries which have witnessed some of the more spectacular increases in output. There are, however, a few important minerals not found in any quantity in these three leading mining countries, notably bauxite and tin.[8] Like much of commercial farming, mining has been developed for the overseas market, and – because of the greater capital required for development – has remained in the hands of a few large enterprises, most of them controlled by foreign financial interests.*

*The great exception is the Oppenheimer empire in the Republic of South Africa controlling De Beers (diamonds) and Anglo-American (gold-mining), as well as much else.

TRANSPORT

In a continent where vast distances still separate the highly productive economic 'islands', and where, as a result, transport is both costly and inefficient, it is of the greatest importance both to reduce costs and to increase efficiency. In the various national development plans so far initiated, between one third and two thirds of all expenditure up to 1959 had gone into the building of roads, railways, and harbour installations,[9] and there is no doubt that much more similar expenditure is still required.

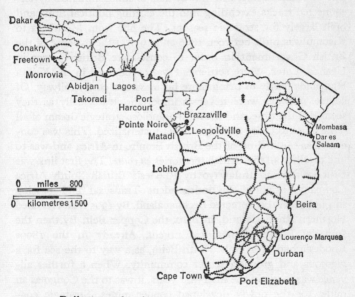

MAP 13. Railways and major ports

The haphazard and uncoordinated development of transport in the past has contributed to the haphazard development of the continent as a whole. Once established, a transport route attracts other forms of investment through the access to markets which it provides. In Senegal the major part of groundnut production is strung out along the railway, as in Gambia it lines the river. Increase the transport facilities, and more farmers would be able to turn from subsistence to commercial farming. In Tanganyika,

on the other hand, one of the factors which led to the choice of
sites for the ill-fated Groundnut Scheme was the existence of a
railway, and it was not until later that the same sites were found
to be unsuitable for groundnut production. This particular railway is a good example of those built for political and strategic
rather than for economic reasons.

The period of greatest activity in railway building – 1890 to
1914 – coincided with the consolidation of European power in
the areas 'allotted' to the various metropolitan countries. Outside of South Africa, the railway map is still dominated by un-
connected tracks extending into the existing political units and
built largely for strategic reasons. The line from Mombasa to
Kisumu was built between 1896 and 1901 at the expense of the
British Government in order to consolidate British power in
Uganda. Later, white settlement was encouraged in the Kenya
Highlands partly to bring more business to a costly railway. Of
course, railways were never as important strategically as they
seemed at the time, and the most grandiose strategic dream of all
– the Cape to Cairo railway – never materialized. This was con-
ceived as the lifeline of the British Empire in Africa and was to
link together all the British territories *en route*. The first link was
built in 1897 to Bulawayo by Rhodes's British South Africa
Company, skirting the independent Transvaal and passing
through recently protected Bechuanaland. By 1905 it had reached
Northern Rhodesia and, in 1910, the Copper Belt. By then the
Imperial Route seemed less urgent. Already in the 1890s
Rhodesia had been linked with Beira, as a way to the sea for a
vigorous and growing settler community. When a further advance was made in the inter-war years, it was to the Congo as an
outlet for the newly developed copper mines. Strategic considerations were beginning to give way to economic ones, although – as with political boundaries – their legacy is still with us.

Two other important facts emerge from the railway map: the
existence of a network of lines only in South Africa and the
very few international links which yet exist. The South African
network is a result of earlier and more intensive economic
development; the international links provide outlets for Zambia,
S. Rhodesia and the Congo. Each of these areas is dependent on

the Portuguese territories for its access to the sea. Even with encouragement from official Belgian sources to use the all-Congo route, it was still cheaper to use the Portuguese railways and ports for more than two thirds of the Katanga trade.

Since the end of the Second World War, roads rather than railways have been built to link the existing lines and to open new areas. The only important railway construction has been undertaken for the export of minerals – iron in Liberia, copper in Uganda, and the new line from Rhodesia to Lourenço Marques built to relieve the congested route to Beira. Apart from these new lines the main effort has been put into roads, and most authorities are agreed that this is the most economical method of transport development at present.[10]

No map of roads is included, because the road 'system' of tropical Africa exists more in the minds of cartographers than as a dependable network on the ground. Bold red lines representing main roads are likely to turn out narrow rutted tracks – adequate for light traffic when it is dry but frequently impassable after heavy rain.[11] The time and material employed in coping with inadequate roads represents an increasingly heavy loss to countries embarking on ambitious development programmes.

DEVELOPMENT FOR THE FUTURE

Economic development up to the standard of European countries can only come with the investment of large sums of capital, which for most of the continent can be expected to yield only a small return. Private capital from the advanced industrial countries is unlikely to be attracted to a low-interest area while there remain more lucrative fields of investment at home. It therefore falls to governments and international lending agencies to make up the deficit.

Only countries with easily exploitable minerals have been able to attract large quantities of private investment, and the uneven distribution of these minerals has been a major cause of the patchy and uneven development to which we have referred.

Before the Second World War investment – both public and private – was heavily concentrated on South Africa, which up to

1936 received nearly half the total of Africa's capital inflow. Table 7 shows the distribution of investment in the rest of Africa south of the Sahara.

TABLE 7

Tropical Africa

Estimated Investment of Capital per head of Population up to 1936

	£ million
Rhodesias	38.4
Belgian Congo	13.0
Angola and Moçambique	*9.8
British East Africa	8.1
British West Africa	4.8
French Colonies	3.3

*Much of this was for port and railway development to serve the Rhodesias and the Belgian Congo.

SOURCE: Lord Hailey, 'African Survey' 1956, p. 1321.

The situation was revolutionized after the war by the decisions of the metropolitan governments to initiate long-term development plans. The British Colonial Development and Welfare Act of 1945 made money available for the individual British territories. The French FIDES* of 1947 aimed at comprehensive planning for France and her dependencies as a single unit, and Belgium initiated a ten-year plan for the Congo in 1950. The Portuguese have launched a series of small-scale development plans since 1938.

French investment, in particular, has increased dramatically since the Second World War. Between 1954 and 1958, public investment in the French Community territories amounted to £14.3 per head of population. For the British territories (excluding the Rhodesias) the comparable figure was £4.1 per head.

Investing Scarce Capital

In investing scarce capital, a choice has often to be made between the large, potentially highly productive but also costly

*Fonds d'Investissement et de Developpement Economique et Social des Territoires d'Outre-Mer. Since 1958, F.A.C. – Fonds d'Aide et de Co-operation.

schemes, and smaller less spectacular projects. These smaller projects may be relatively less productive in potential, but frequently cost less and bring quicker returns to the participants. One such scheme is the recent agrarian reform in Kenya, much of which has been promoted as a by-product of security needs during and after the Mau Mau Emergency.

Kikuyuland is a fertile, well-watered area in the Kenya Highlands. During this century over-population, over-stocking, and primitive farming methods had all helped to bring about a deterioration of soil and an increase in discontent.* In the Fort Hall and Kiambu districts there are population densities of over 350 to the square mile, an extremely high figure for a rural area. As well as soil erosion, low productivity resulted from the excessive fragmentation of holdings.

Prior to the Emergency, the Kikuyu lived in scattered settlements. Part of the security measures during the Mau Mau rebellion was the forcible 'villagization' of the Kikuyu and the consolidation of fragmented holdings. In addition, under the Swynnerton Plan of 1954, £10m was invested in the improvement of farming methods and the introduction of cash crops. As a result the face of Kikuyuland has been transformed. Now there are not only villages where none existed before, but rows of crops and trees planted along the contour, cultivated terraces, and farmers who are enjoying a cash income for the first time in their lives. The density of population is at last being matched by the intensive cultivation of available land.

Elspeth Huxley has described the working of the scheme:

A typical planned small-holding of from ten to twenty acres will have cash crops like coffee, pyrethrum, and pineapples, together with some grazing for livestock, fodder, and food crops. Most of the small-holders have adopted the officially approved farm plan or lay-out.

Farm lay-outs are not compulsory, but in the Central Province, where everyone was moved into a village during the Emergency and needed permission to move out while it lasted (October 1952 to January 1960), farmers were not normally able to settle until they had accepted the principle of these simple plans. . . .

A farm lay-out will suggest to you where to put your homestead

*It is not suggested that the discontent was entirely economic. There were many political grievances and much justified opposition to the *enforcement* of the improvements outlined below.

and sheds, to site your paddocks on the contour, the best place for a
firewood plantation ... where to grow your food. The basic principle
is that all arable land should spend about half its life under grass,
generally on a seven- or eight-year cycle.

This may sound simple, and so it is, but to people brought up in
the practice of shifting cultivation it is revolutionary.[12]

There is much to criticize in Kenya land reform – compulsion,
too little attention to marketing, and too few jobs for the land-
less. When individual ownership of land has replaced tribal
ownership, the owner-occupier may become richer in the process, but his poor relations find it increasingly difficult to live off
his production and end up by helping to swell the army of un-
employed in the towns. The improvements are, however, small
enough to be well-understood, and their results have not been
too remote in time. Other examples of successful small-scale
land improvements are the *paysannat* schemes of French Equatorial Africa, which aim at settling peasant farmers on land newly
cleared for them by government agency. One such scheme that
has worked well is the Mandingou *paysannat* in the Niari valley
of ex-French Congo.

A score or so of villages, comprising several hundred families, have
been established on good soils, and in close proximity to both the
road and railroad linking Brazzaville and Pointe Noire. Each village
is surrounded by, or adjacent to, a number of fields that the administering authority has had mechanically cleared and ploughed. These
fields may be anything up to 100 or 150 acres in size. Each family with
two working adults has been given approximately seven acres of
arable land.... This land they sow and cultivate by hand as directed
by their supervisors. The crops grown are the peanut ... sweet
potato, urena (a fibre that has all the uses of hemp and some others
besides), manioc, maize, and a variety of green crops for ploughing
under; they are grown according to a strict four-year rotation. In
addition to the arable land each family has been given a pig and about
half an acre of land for coffee.

As the Mandingou Scheme was begun only in 1955 it is still too
early to pass judgement on it. But the prospects of success seem
good.[13]

Large-scale Development

The first of the spectacular improvement plans to reach the news headlines in the post-war world was the *Groundnut Scheme* in Tanganyika. In conception it was an attempt to have the best of all possible worlds; to combine the pre-war notion of Africa as a supplier of Europe's food and raw materials with the post-war notion of development for the sake of African advancement. Twenty-five million pounds was allotted to the original scheme in 1948, and it was aimed to produce over 500,000 tons of groundnuts annually within five to six years.

Speed on a large scale was deemed to be essential, although it proved to be the chief cause of failure. It was thought necessary to increase the supply of fat to food-rationed Britain, and the heavy political opposition to the scheme demanded a spectacular political success. Three sites were selected after only a hurried examination of soils, climate, terrain, and communications, and it was not really surprising that the scheme turned out a costly failure, a gamble that did not come off. Drought, bush clearance, difficulties of soil cultivation, and the blunting of mechanical tools were some of the many natural difficulties encountered, and by 1951 the scheme had to be reduced to the pilot project that it ought to have been in the first place. This has done invaluable research work on the problems of commercial farming in the three areas.[14] A glance at Map 22 illustrates one of the difficulties which could have been avoided if the information had been obtained before the scheme started. Not one of the three chosen areas lies within the region where there is even a fair prospect of receiving thirty inches of rainfall each year. The *East African Royal Commission Report* (1955), from which the map is adapted, notes that the areas where there is little prospect of obtaining thirty inches (areas in which Kongwa and Nachingwea are situated), 'are those where the reliability of a thirty-inch rainfall is too poor to allow arable farming to be normally possible'. The areas where there is a poor or a fair prospect of obtaining thirty inches (in which Urambo is situated) 'are those where the indifferent reliability of a thirty-inch rainfall produces marginal conditions of a kind which do not necessarily preclude arable farming, but which place distinct limitations upon the likelihood of its success. . .'[15]

The Volta River Project in Ghana

A number of factors have combined to make the large-scale development of river valleys appear the key to rapid economic growth in a number of African countries. The plateau edge which led to isolation in the past can provide the key to future development of cheap hydro-electric power, as has already been achieved at Owen Falls in Uganda and at Kariba in Rhodesia. Concurrently with the provision of power can go essential water control and conservation. There is, too, the experience and enthusiasm of American and other foreign engineers who have helped in similar large-scale development at home and whose ideas have been influential in the drawing up of preliminary plans. Finally, the spectacular nature of many of the schemes finds favour with governments for political reasons, either because they may provide quick popularity at home or because they may attract more investment capital from abroad.

The Volta river project was first mooted in 1924, and various plans have been drawn up from time to time – the last in 1959 – to provide for the construction of a large dam across the Volta river at Akosombo. The resulting lake would be enormous, stretching for some 300 miles across half the length of Ghana and influencing the whole of the surrounding area.

Initially the plan has four main purposes – the provision of an aluminium smelter near the dam site for which power is not at present available, the further development of bauxite mining, the improvement of transport facilities, and the irrigation of part of the Accra plains. The new port of Tema is now finished, and work has begun on the dam, hydro-electric station, and the aluminium smelter. The project, as planned, will be expensive and spectacular, both economically and politically. It will enable Ghana not only to maintain but to increase her lead in living standards, as well as helping her to support her claim to political leadership among African states.

The Kariba Dam

The Kariba Dam is not a plan but a reality, and a highly publicized one as well. Begun in 1954, it was finished in June 1959, and Lake Kariba – 175 miles long – has been full since early 1962. Development of the ancillary power stations and transmission lines is due for completion in 1972. It is, of course, a great achievement, both for the engineers and workmen who built it and for the government which was able to finance it. It will undoubtedly bring great benefits to Zambia and Rhodesia in the future – cheap power for the further development of mining and manufacturing, water conservation for irrigation and other purposes, and fishing to provide much-needed protein foods. But these are still future benefits, and the dam at present is still only a wonderful piece of window-dressing to catch the attention of the outside world, both politicians and investors. It has not yet improved the lives of many individuals, and like other large schemes it has been immensely costly in scarce capital. It may help to attract further investment, but will certainly postpone some of the immediate benefits which might have accrued from smaller and less expensive schemes. For a government so precariously placed at home, an improvement in the lives of the people it is supposed to serve might have been thought more important than impressing the outside world.

Before Kariba was begun 'a decision had to be taken between the two great schemes for hydro-electric power, Kariba and Kafue. Kariba was the bigger, the more expensive and the slower ... (but) ... by the time Kafue was finished more power would be needed'. Kafue was also a wholly Northern Rhodesian scheme, and Kariba is on the border between the two countries. 'So sharp was the controversy between these two bodies of opinion that little was heard in Rhodesia of a third view, that a much higher priority, perhaps at the expense of these schemes, should have been given to plans for putting money directly into the pockets of African farmers by irrigation and cooperative marketing'.[16] Investment will not be attracted to a government unless it is seen to be economically progressive; nor will it be attracted to one with serious political unrest on its hands.

This brief consideration of the three schemes outlined here

points a number of lessons for the future. Of these the first and most important is the need for adequate information and for the preliminary research necessary to acquire it. If the development really cannot wait on careful preliminary planning, then the small scheme which is also a pilot project runs less danger of being a spectacular failure – either economic or political – than the large venture. In any event, experiment will be required as well as planning, and we may need to challenge some fundamental assumptions in the process. For example, it was thought until quite recently that the use of large tsetse-infested areas to produce animal protein necessarily required the elimination of fly and the improvement of animal husbandry. Now it has been shown that

over much of Africa's wild land a given area will produce a larger weight of animal protein – meat – and might be made to yield a larger financial profit, if cropped for game – that is to say by killing surplus wild animals for meat or hides – than through the medium of cattle or any domestic stock.[17]

Another lesson for the future is the need for the right political conditions. In Ghana, careful publicity and an African government have produced a climate of opinion favourable to the success of the Volta project. It is, in addition, a scheme which has received much careful preparatory planning. Kariba on the other hand, while a technical success, has been a political success only abroad and among the Rhodesian Europeans, not among the Africans. Future benefits seem to them less important than present needs.[18]

Finally, we must not forget that the large schemes may themselves help to accentuate the uneven economic development of the continent which we have already noted. Large schemes need a great deal of money to implement, and much of this will have to come from commercial sources. Countries which have readily exploitable minerals or confident European minorities may well find it easier to attract scarce capital than those whose obvious natural resources are less. In east Africa for example, the contrast between development on Mt Kilimanjaro or in Buganda and such areas as the West Nile district of Uganda is greater than the contrast between farming areas of Western Europe and the former regions. Again, within individual territories un-balanced economies need to be balanced. Ghana needs the industrial development which the Volta project will bring, but Ghana's neighbours need to be brought up to her standards. The Rhodesias desperately need investment in agriculture as well as in an industry which has already outpaced the subsistence economy. 'Attention needs to be given to the underdeveloped areas within the underdeveloped whole.'[19]

Our state of knowledge about Africa's economic potential is such that we are still in the stage of asking questions and of looking for the right questions to ask, rather than having ready answers to those which have occurred. It is important that this is recognized because then there may still be time for Africa to develop both profitably and peacefully. As we noted in Chapter I, there is still space in Africa, space to grow, to develop and to increase the richness of human choice. The population explosion is only just beginning there. By the time it really gets under way the answers should have been found.

Notes on Chapter 4

1. See Chapter 12 below.
2. For a full discussion of population distribution see P. Gourou, *The Tropical World*, 2nd ed., 1958, pp. 83–5.
3. W. A. Hance, *African Economic Development*, p. 5.
4. U.N. *Economic Survey of Africa since 1950*, pp. 99–114.
5. J. Phillips, *Agriculture and Ecology in Africa: a Study of Actual and Potential Development South of the Sahara*, 1959, p. 376.
6. Known coal reserves are mainly confined to the Republic of South Africa and Southern Rhodesia. The whole continent contains less than 1 per cent of probable world coal reserves and less than 2 per cent of proved oil reserves. The production of coal per annum between 1955 and 1957 was:

South Africa	33,503,000 tons
Southern Rhodesia	3,574,000 tons
Nigeria	796,000 tons
Congo	444,000 tons

U.N. *Economic Survey of Africa since 1950*, p. 132.

7. Counting Congo (ex-Belgian), Ruanda and Burundi together.
8. U.N., op. cit., pp. 61–6.
9. *United Africa Company, Statistical & Economic Review.* Special issue on Transport in Africa, March 1961, p. 4.
10. United Africa Co., op. cit., and W. A. Hance, op. cit., pp. 116–7.
11. Hance, op. cit., p. 116.
12. E. Huxley, *A New Earth*, 1960, p. 212–13.

13. G. H. T. Kimble, *Tropical Africa*, 1960, Vol. I., p. 178.

14. The scheme is more fully considered in Phillips, op. cit., Chap. 32.

15. *East Africa Royal Commission 1953–5 Report*, 1955 (Cmd. 9477), p. 254.

16. Philip Mason, *Year of Decision*, 1960, p. 57.

17. Sir Julian Huxley, 'Cropping the Wild Protein', Article in the *Observer*, 20 November 1960, p. 23.

18. *Monckton Commission Report*, p. 135.

19. Hance, op. cit., p. 286.

See in addition, L. P. Green and T. J. D. Fair, *Development in Africa*, Witwatersrand University Press, Johannesburg, 1962. Many African countries now have reports on their economic development prepared by the International Bank for Reconstruction and Development. Examples are *The Economic Development of Uganda* (1961) and *The Economic Development of Kenya* (1962). In most cases comprehensive government development plans have been prepared and published after consideration of these reports.

Part II Regional Studies

West Africa

West Africa is the home of some of the finest achievements of the early Negro civilizations. It has also been able to advance most rapidly towards political independence in the mid-twentieth century. Partly this is because the climate has not encouraged much white settlement, so that educational and economic advance for Africans has not been impeded by the presence of an alien and privileged settler community. Here, too, there has been specialization on a number of tropical crops like cocoa and the oil palm. This, unlike the exploitation of minerals, has brought wealth to thousands of small cultivators rather than to huge industrial companies.

West Africa is, however, the area which has suffered most from the political fragmentation imposed by Europeans, where boundaries were settled with the least regard for the physical and human divisions of the area, and where, in consequence, political advance accompanies the most acute political rivalries.

The area comprises the states of former French West Africa,* the former mandated territory of Togoland, Portuguese Guinea, Liberia, Gambia, Sierra Leone, Ghana, and Nigeria. With more than ninety million people, it contains nearly half the population of tropical Africa. Also included in this study are the Spanish territories and the transitional thinly peopled largely forest zone of former French Equatorial Africa (Chad, Central African Republic, Congo, and Gabon), and Cameroun, containing another nine million people speaking mainly Bantu languages.

The great contrast in West Africa is between the southern forest zone and the northern savanna lands. The forest has here been the area of difficulty – difficult to penetrate and difficult to settle without the importation of alien food crops. In the

*Mauritania, Mali, Niger, Senegal, Guinea, Ivory Coast, Dahomey, and Upper Volta.

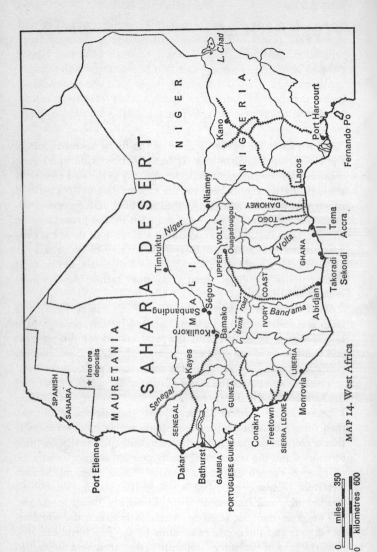

MAP 14. West Africa

savanna lands, on the other hand, movement was easy and native food plants were available to sustain a relatively large population. Eastwards from Senegal, through Mali and Upper Volta to Northern Nigeria, lies a belt of relatively high population density in which a number of important states developed during the medieval period, of which Ghana from the ninth to the eleventh centuries and Mali in the fourteenth century were the most important.

Not only did these savanna states have the advantages of easy movement and adequate native food plants, but, from the first century A.D., they were in regular and sustained contact with Mediterranean civilization. Trade in goods and ideas was carried across the Sahara by camel caravan, and the stimulus of this contact was an important source of progress.

This early supremacy of the savanna country began to be reversed in the sixteenth century, when West Europeans finally broke the Arab monopoly of trade with the Guinea coast. The trans-Saharan caravan routes decayed and the coastal forest zone was henceforth the area in greatest contact with the outside world; contact which was often destructive but which eventually led to the emergence on the coast of an educated African *élite* and the beginnings of modern economic development. Both these events have been of considerable significance in the emergence of independent west African states.

In the chapters on west Africa which follow, the conventional academic treatment of west Africa as an entity has been avoided. Now that almost the whole region has emerged into political independence, there is an even greater likelihood than before that both economic and political development will proceed – for some time to come – within the existing national units. It is therefore important to consider the present political groupings separately rather than to treat the region as the unit which historically and in terms of physical geography it is.

Nigeria is taken on its own, partly because it is so large and partly because it provides something of a cross-section of the whole area. Ghana, Guinea, and Mali, the 'radical' states, are treated as an entity, while the remaining two chapters in this section are devoted to the rest of English-speaking and the rest of former French Africa.

5 Nigeria: Cross-Section of the West

In size, variety of peoples and environments, as well as in the challenges which these present for future development, Nigeria in many ways exemplifies the problems of tropical Africa as a whole. Size and human variety set problems of political cohesion. There are the usual problems of water supply, poor soils, and disease, while the general level of poverty is as low as anywhere in Africa. Stretching from the dense forests of the south to the margins of the Sahara, Nigeria provides therefore a revealing cross-section of west African life, in many ways typical of the whole region.

Size and the variety of its environments do, however, give it advantages denied to many of its neighbours. The economy of the whole is varied, and the unity imposed by British rule at least turns regional differences into internal political problems rather than matters of international relations.

The third-largest territory in area and the largest in population, Nigeria is bound to exert tremendous influence on its neighbours. It is a land some four times the size of the United Kingdom and has between fifty and sixty million people. The fact that its independence is so recent means that this influence has only just begun to be felt, but already Nigeria has a place of substantial importance among independent African states.

MAJOR TRIBAL GROUPINGS

Nigeria at the time of independence was a federation with three strong regional governments and a federal government to cover all three regions. Each of the original regions is the core area of one or other of the major tribal groups – Hausa in the North, Yoruba in the West, and Ibo in the East – though on region was linguistically or culturally homogeneous.

Prior to independence there was considerable local pressure for many more regions, and no less than fifteen were demanded at the 1957 London Conference. These demands were successfully resisted, however, and the constitutional difficulties of creating new regions were made fairly formidable.* These difficulties were overcome in 1963 in the case of the new Mid-West Region.

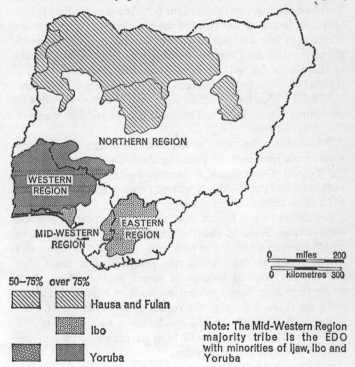

MAP 15. Tribal nuclei and regional boundaries

This new region consists of the Delta and Benin provinces formerly belonging to the West, and has as its capital the ancient city of Benin. It is a product both of local opposition to Yoruba domination and of the 1962–3 political crisis in the Western

*(a) Two thirds majority in favour in both federal houses.
  (b) Approval by a majority of Houses of Assembly of the existing regions.
  (c) A referendum with 60 per cent of the new state's registered voters approving.

Region. This crisis brought defeat to the Action Group government there and enabled the National Council of Nigerian Citizens (N.C.N.C.) to press successfully for the creation of the new region. The N.C.N.C. now forms the regional government in the Mid-West as it still does in the East.[1]

More than three quarters of the population in the West is Yoruba-speaking, two thirds of the population in the East is Ibo-speaking, and about one third of the population in the North has Hausa as its first language, the use of which is constantly spreading in the Region. There are considerable minorities of Yoruba in the North (as well as in neighbouring Dahomey), and if regional divisions grow these could become focuses of discontent.

The Mid-West has no ethnic unity except in the sense that its population is non-Yoruba. The main groups are Edo-speakers, Ibo, Ika, and Ijaw.

The North – according to the last census figures – contains rather more than half the total population, and in consequence the Federal Government is largely dominated by the third major political party – the Northern People's Congress – which as its name implies is a regional group.

Population census figures in Nigeria have important political implications. Seats in the Federal House of Representatives are allocated on a population basis and, with political parties still largely based on the regions, the census figures could alter radically the political balance of power between them. As a result, there have been two census counts in Nigeria in the last few years (1962 and 1963), the results of which have both been in dispute.* The 1963 figures are, however, accepted as official and mean that the North will keep its preponderance in the Federal House of Representatives.[2]

*1963 Census Figures
  North 29,777,986
  East 12,388,646
  West 10,278,500
  Mid-West 2,533,337
  Lagos 675,352
  Total. 55,653,821
  Source: *The Times*, 26 February 1964.

TABLE 8

Nigeria: Tribal Groups in the 1952 Population Census

Tribe	Total (in 000s)	N. Region per cent	E. Region per cent	W. Region per cent
Hausa	5,547	99	—*	—
Ibo	5,482	3	91	6
Yoruba	5,046	10	1	89
Fulani	3,040	99	—	—
Kanuri	1,301	99	—	—
Tiv	789	97	3	—
Ibibio	765	2	97	1

* — Shows less than 1 per cent.

Figures for the Eastern Region include Southern Cameroons, a U.N. Trust Territory formerly administered as part of Nigeria and now joined with independent Cameroun.

As will be seen from the table, the Hausa do not dominate numerically in the North to anything like the same extent as do Yoruba and Ibo in West and East respectively. This greater tribal diversity in the North is, however, offset by the greater cultural homogeneity which comes from the practice of Islam. Only the so-called Middle Belt, the southern part of the Northern Region, does not have a Moslem majority, and this is a much less heavily populated area than either the rest of the region or the other two regions.

HISTORICAL OUTLINE

Both the Northern and Western Regions have a long tradition of political and military organization.

In the North, the Hausa States arose from the twelfth century onwards, becoming converted to Islam in the fourteenth century as a result of contacts with traders and missionaries from Mali to the west.[3] They were then brought under the rule of one political system with the Fulani revolution of the early nineteenth century.

The Fulani, a cattle-keeping nomadic people (in contradistinction to the crop-growing Hausa), had been moving into the Hausa states since the fifteenth century, frequently constituting an intellectual and religious *élite* whose reforming zeal seems to have been the main cause of the Fulani seizure of political power. In consequence a large region formerly the preserve of a number of independent states was brought under a single government. And it was not only the Hausa states which were brought under Fulani rule. The new empire was able to extend its frontiers as far south as the Benue river in the east, and south of the Niger well into the Yoruba areas of the west, bringing with it for the first time an extension of Islamic religious influence. Hodgkin takes the view that

European commentators have tended to underestimate the extent to which the Fulani Empire survived through the nineteenth century as an effective political unit. It was, of course, a state of a broadly 'feudal' type, in which the various provincial governors ... enjoyed a large autonomy, and revolted from time to time against the central power; but it remained discernibly a state.[4]

When a British protectorate was established over Northern Nigeria in 1900, much of the existing political structure was retained under a system of 'indirect rule'. The northern Emirs, together with their councillors and officials, became officials of the new native administration.

One important consequence of the treaties made by the British Government with the Moslem Emirs was that Christian missions were in general not allowed into the exclusively Moslem areas. As a great deal of the educational system has been in the hands of the missions, there is now a considerable contrast in standards of literacy between the North and the two southern regions. In the North, literacy in Roman script is under 5 per cent outside of the Yoruba minority areas and the non-Moslem tribes of the Jos plateau, while literacy in Hausa (Arabic script) is nowhere greater than 15 per cent. Literacy rates in both the West and the East are up to 25 per cent in many areas, but only in parts of the Eastern Region is this figure exceeded. One result of this contrast in literacy standards has been the importation into the Northern Region of clerks and others from among the southern tribes, an importation which is resented by many traditionalist rulers in the North, particularly since it has been accompanied by radical pressures.

The Yoruba States – of which the chief were Oyo and Benin – arose between the eleventh and fourteenth centuries. From the seventeenth century onwards secular power was predominantly in the hands of the Alafin of Oyo, while both Oyo and Benin accepted the spiritual authority of the Oni of Ife. By the nineteenth century the Yoruba States were in decline. Fulani expan-

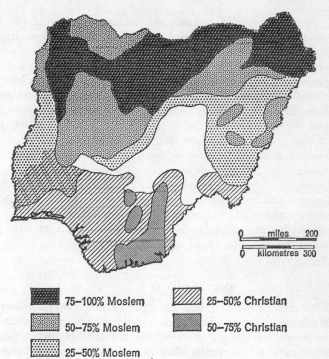

75–100% Moslem   25–50% Christian

50–75% Moslem   50–75% Christian

25–50% Moslem

MAP 16. The frontiers of Islam and Christianity. (Modified from J. Spencer Trimingham, *Islam in Africa*, 1959)

sion had detached some of the more northerly areas, while pressure from Dahomey in the west and the depredations of the slave trade had reduced political stability and cohesion in the region.

The Ibo have no such tradition of political and military organization, and before the establishment of British rule were organized in small family and kinship groups. Perhaps this is one reason why Christian missions have had more success in the Eastern Region than elsewhere in Nigeria. Only here are there areas with over half the population Christian.[5] Attempts to rule the Ibo areas through native authorities were not successful, because there were no suitable native authorities through which to rule.

British occupation was achieved piecemeal from the 1860s onwards. Lagos was occupied in 1861 and a Colony created there in the following year. The Oil Rivers Protectorate was established in 1885 in the region of the Niger delta, being re-named the Niger Coast Protectorate in 1893. Then in 1899 control passed from the Foreign to the Colonial Office, and the Protectorate of Southern Nigeria was formed in the following year. In the same year the responsibilities of the Royal Niger Company to the north were taken over by the British Government and a Protectorate declared over Northern Nigeria. Government in both protectorates, however, was not completely effective for another nine or ten years. The last partly independent areas were not absorbed until 1914, when the whole country was brought under one administration and the unified Colony and Protectorate of Nigeria began its history under the Governor Generalship of Lord Lugard.

THE PHYSICAL ENVIRONMENT

With most of the country lying under 2,000 ft above sea level, Nigeria is everywhere a hot country to live in, having in common with most of the rest of west Africa a climate which most Europeans find enervating. There is a gradual increase in height of the plateau surfaces from south to north, but this has little effect on temperature except on the central Jos plateau, parts of which rise to over 4,000 ft.

The south has the smallest range of temperature, both between day and night and between the hottest and coolest months. Moving north the daily range increases, as do the differences between the hottest and coolest months, so that the north experiences both the hottest days and the coolest nights.

TABLE 9

Temperature Contrasts in Nigeria.

	Mean Monthly Maxima	Mean Monthly Minima
Calabar (in the south-east)	81.6 to 89.4	72.3 to 74.5
Nguru (in the north-east)	87.3 to 103.6	53.8 to 74.3

Source: K. M. Buchanan and J. C. Pugh, *Land and People in Nigeria,* 1955, p. 30.

Nigeria is typical of Africa as a whole in that rainfall and water supply are far more significant than temperature in limiting or stimulating human activities. Rainfall exceeds 120 inches along parts of the south-east coast, but the amount falls away rapidly to north and west, where large areas have only between 20 and 40 inches. More important than the crude annual totals is the northward increase in the length of the dry season, so that areas which may seem to have quite comfortable annual totals have, for at least part of the year, insufficient water in the soil for the growth of crops. Even Calabar in the south-east has a period of two months when moisture loss from the soil is greater than rainfall, although it receives over 100 inches annually and there is no month which is completely dry. It must be concluded from this that there are few parts of the country and indeed of the whole of West Africa where full use can be made of favourable growth temperatures without irrigation. Over more than half of Nigeria the annual need for water is greater than the rainfall. This assessment pays no regard to the requirement of animal stocks, human consumption, and industry. Long-term development will clearly have to include major irrigation schemes on the Niger and Benue.[6]

THE SUBSISTENCE ECONOMY

The fundamental contrast in subsistence agriculture is that between the grain economy of the north and the root economy of the south. These represent adaptations to a grassland and a forest environment respectively. There is some overlapping in the Middle Belt, but this is away from the main areas of dense population. In the southern root economy, yams and cassava are the main crops, with subsidiary rice and beans, while, especially in the south-east, the oil palm is important in both subsistence and commercial agriculture. Over most of the country cultivation is by the normal African bush fallowing system, and one part of Yoruba country has been described as follows:

> The area is cleared in February and ... burned soon after ... The main crops of yams and corn are planted with the first rains together with pumpkins, melons and calabashes. When the first corn* is harvested in June, beans, cassava, okra and cocoyams may be planted. A second crop of corn is planted in August and harvested in October or November; yams are harvested in September or October.[7]

The fallow period in this area may be from eight to fourteen years, but in parts of Ibo country has been dangerously reduced as a result of population pressure.

The northern grain economy is devoted mainly to millets and sorghums, with guinea corn as a subsidiary crop and groundnuts on the lighter soils. Around the larger towns more permanent cultivation has been developed, associated with the availability of animal manure, light, easily worked soils, and wells and streams for irrigation. The most extensive area of this type is around the city of Kano.

POPULATION DISTRIBUTION

The three main areas of high density roughly correspond with the three main tribal nuclei, and also with those areas which are the major contributors to commercial agriculture. In between the high density areas of north and south lies the thinly populated middle belt, comprising two fifths of the country's area, which has only one fifth of the population. Poor soils, low rainfall and scanty ground water have contributed to poverty in population and wealth. Even more important, probably, have been centuries of slave-raiding and warfare, both from north and south. With a population constantly reduced in this way, tsetse-infested bush country had been able to encroach on once cultivated land, making it all the more difficult to settle again once warfare and slaving ceased for a while. The existence

*i.e. maize.

today of this wide, thinly peopled area between north and south helps to emphasize the differences between the Moslem north and the other two regions.

High densities in parts of the north have been facilitated by the light, easily worked soils, good ground water supplies for irrigation, and the absence of tsetse fly. Strategic position on the

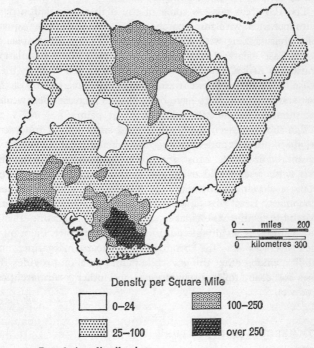

Density per Square Mile

☐	0–24	▨	100–250
▨	25–100	■	over 250

MAP 17. Population distribution

trans-Saharan caravan routes has also been important, as has the political stability provided by powerful empires. In recent years the coming of the railway has provided the necessary outlet to the sea for the development of commercial agriculture and a consequent increase in wealth and population.

A more powerful political organization than their neighbours have enjoyed also helped the Yoruba to maintain their numbers in spite of slave-raiding – numbers increased in recent years with the opportunities provided by the growing of cash crops like cocoa. The Yoruba areas of the Western Region are characterized by a high concentration of people in large towns, unusual elsewhere in rural Africa. Ibadan, with half a million people (about the size of Leeds), ranks as the largest purely African city in Tropical Africa.

The Ibo areas possess some of the highest population densities in Africa, with some patches of 1,500 people to the square mile, thus ranking with some of the highly populated areas of South-East Asia and approaching a degree of over-population unusual in Africa. The Ibo seem to have been protected by their dense forest environment from some of the slave raiding of the past and in recent years have been able to increase their wealth and numbers by the cultivation of the oil palm.

The Ibo have been fortunate in this, since – apart from sensitivity to drought and waterlogging – the oil palm is tolerant in its soil requirements. Most of the cultivation consists in looking after wild or semi-wild trees, and in the Eastern Region the oil palm is dominant in both the subsistence and the export economies. Leaf ribs and leaves are used in building and thatching; palm wine makes a pleasant intoxicating drink, and palm oil is a valuable addition to the local diet. Palm oil is used overseas for the production of soap, margarine, and candles, among other things; while palm kernel oil provides the basis for soap, toilet preparations, and other pharmaceutical products.

COMMERCIAL AGRICULTURE

The wealth of Nigeria lies mainly in agriculture, which occupies at least 80 per cent of the working population and supplies some 60 per cent of the national income. Commercial farming occupies about one quarter of the land under cultivation and is concentrated in three main areas of dense population. Each area, with its distinctive natural environment, is characterized by different export crops: cotton and groundnuts in the North, cocoa in the Yoruba areas of the West, and palm oil and kernels in the Ibo East.

The dependence of each region on one or two export crops is typical of the smaller independent countries of west Africa. United in one political unit, they become complementary to each other and a source of national strength. With the exception of cocoa, there is considerable local consumption of these crops

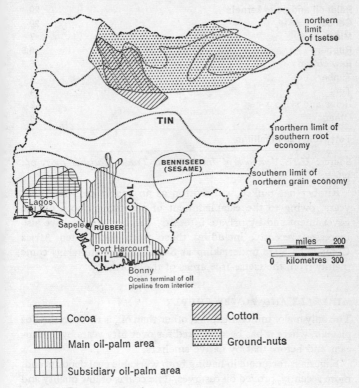

MAP 18. Export production areas

and, as a result, considerable local trade between the three regions. The Middle Belt at present provides a small food surplus for export to the other areas, a surplus which should be increased in any future agricultural expansion. There is little plantation agriculture, and most of the export production is in the hands of smallholders.

TABLE IO

Nigeria: Exports in 1961 (by value)

	per cent
Groundnuts (and oil)	22
Palm oil and palm kernels	20
Cocoa	20
Mineral oil	7
Rubber	6.5
Raw cotton	6.5
Timber	4
Tin	4
Hides and skins	2
Other	8

Total value £170 million

Source: *U.N. Yearbook of International Trade Statistics 1961*, pp. 476–7.

Rubber has ranked with cotton as an export crop in recent years, owing to the establishment of plantations both by the government and by private interests. Timber exports have also increased recently, including those from the United Africa Company's huge undertaking at Sapele. Hides and skins come mainly from the tsetse-free areas of the North.

MINERALS AND POWER SUPPLY

The only major mineral export, other than oil, is tin from the Jos plateau, where it has been worked for over fifty years by Europeans and before that by native smelters.

Nigeria is fortunate in having both workable coal deposits and, more recently, proved oil reserves. The coal is of low quality and is used mainly on the railways and for electricity production, but both uses are important in a country which has not yet developed hydro-electricity to any extent, except on the Jos Plateau for the use of the tin industry. Total production amounts to rather less than 1 million tons annually.

High-cost coal production is not likely to increase in the future, since lower-cost oil output is now expected to grow. Though it was first produced in exportable quantities no earlier than 1958, heavy investments have now been made in the oilfield of the Niger delta. Production reached over two million tons in 1961 and there is a planned expansion programme to 4½ million tons by 1965. The work has been undertaken by the Shell-B.P. Petroleum Development Co. of Nigeria, which shares the profits with the government on a fifty-fifty basis.

TRANSPORT

At least 30 per cent of current development plan money is being spent on the improvement of railways, roads, harbours and water transport. The railway system is still only single-track and, like most other African railways, is now heavily overloaded. Road traffic, especially of commercial vehicles, has increased enormously in recent years, but only a few trunk roads have tarred surfaces and many are impassable in the wet season.

With the improvement of inland transport arrangements, port installations already working at peak capacity will have to be improved. Lagos handles over twice as much cargo as the other major port, Port Harcourt, and in both there are already costly delays in the turn-round of ships because of congestion. The improvement of Port Harcourt is complicated by the shifting and constantly silting channels of the Niger delta, improvements to which are now in hand.

Most important for the future of Nigeria will be the development of the Niger and Benue rivers. These rivers, so impressive on the map, are not as yet the aid to trade and movement which they will become in the future. Up till now they have served rather to divide than to unite the country, and they need to be improved for navigation, for irrigation, and for power supplies, the more so because such a large part of their course lies in the under-populated and relatively neglected Middle Belt.

Research work on river improvement was started by a Dutch firm in 1953, and as a result the Escravos* scheme for improving navigational outlets in the Niger delta has been approved by the Federal Government and is due for completion in 1964. The same Dutch firm also investigated possibilities along both the

*Named after the major outlet proposed.

Niger and the Benue and published its most comprehensive report in 1959.[8]

Both rivers are seasonal and irregular in flow, and any scheme must consist of a series of dams to impound flood water and provide a controlled discharge for both navigation and irrigation, as well as the necessary head of water for the generation of power. A site has now been selected by the Federal Government for a multi-purpose dam on the Niger at Kurwasa, north of Jebba. The scheme as at present outlined is likely to cost at least £55 millions; but if the capital investment is forthcoming, it could be completed by 1966. The careful preparatory research work for the project has been one of the most thorough investigations ever carried out on one of the world's great rivers.

Large size and population, regional variety and divisions, and the usual problems of developing a backward economy in a difficult tropical environment: these are the most important facts to remember in considering Nigeria's future role. The country is large enough and varied enough to develop on its own, and it has sufficient political divisions within its own borders not to wish to enlarge its territory (and its problems) by union with others.

Notes on Chapter 5

1. D. B. Abernethy, '*Nigeria Creates a New Region*', in *Africa Report*, March 1964.
2. J. P. Mackintosh, 'How Many Nigerians?'. in *New Statesman*, 13 March 1964, pp. 390–92.
3. T. Hodgkin, *Nigerian Perspectives*, 1960, p. 23.
4. ibid., p. 41.
5. See the map of religious distribution in J. Spencer Trimingham, *Islam in West Africa*, 1959.
6. B. J. Garnier, *The Moisture Resources of Nigeria and their Utilization* in *Natural Resources in Tropical Africa*. Report of a symposium held at Makerere College, 1955.
7. P. A. Allinson 'From Farm to Forest', in *Farm and Forest* Vol. II, No. 2 (1941), pp. 95–6. Quoted in K. M. Buchanan and J. C. Pugh, *Land and People in Nigeria*, 1955, p. 105. This is the best single book on Nigerian geography.
8. *River Studies and Recommendations on the Improvements of the Niger and the Benue*, by N.E.D.E.C.O, 1959.
   In addition the following are recommended.
   R. J. Harrison Church, *West Africa*, 1957, Chap. 26.
   G. B. Stapleton, *The Wealth of Nigeria*, 1958.
   R.I.I.A., *Nigeria: the Political and Economical Background*, 1960.

6 Ghana, Guinea, and Mali

These three states of West Africa, politically radical in complexion and linked together in a loose – largely paper – political union for a short while from December 1960, emerged into independence at different times and by reason of different decisions made by their leaders and rulers.

Ghana was the first African state to achieve independence in the post-war world as a result of successful nationalist pressure against British rule. Guinea suddenly became independent two years later by virtue of her unique 'No' vote in the French referendum of 1958. Mali, the former French Sudan, after an abortive federation with Senegal,* became fully independent in August 1960.

At the time of Guinea's independence in 1958, the annual subsidy of £6 million from France was withdrawn. Ghana came forward with a loan of £10 million to help overcome the immediate financial problem, coupling this with the offer of a political union. In December 1960 the union was extended to include Mali.

The union remained, however, more an expression of intention than a reality. The three were drawn together by a common ideology – they are Pan-Africanist and neutralist in foreign policy, are 'one-party democracies' in internal political organization, and possess complementary economies. Two of them (Ghana and Guinea) have developing mineral resources and one (Mali) has a food surplus. Ghana, the richest state in West Africa, has already been able to extend a token amount of financial aid to the other two. There were, however, many obstacles in the way of a real political union among them.

First, they are not geographically contiguous. Even the links

*The federation lasted for only a few months during 1960, negotiated its independence from France and also bore the name Mali.

between Mali and Guinea are tenuous, as there is neither railway nor adequate road between them. The railway from Mali to Senegal is the traditional route to the sea from Mali, a route which political divisions closed for a time and which it would be difficult and costly to replace.

Secondly, Guinea and Mali are both predominantly Moslem, and have French as a common language. Ghana is not a Moslem country, uses English instead of French, and is the only one of the three to be in the sterling area and a member of the Common- wealth.

MALI has at least one town which everyone can recognize – Timbuktu. Like Kano in Nigeria, this ancient city owed its importance to its situation astride the trans-Saharan caravan routes and the existence of available water for irrigated agricul- ture. This combination of circumstances also helps to explain the rise in the same area of medieval Mali, from which the modern state is named, and which reached the peak of its power in the thirteenth and fourteenth centuries.

French penetration from Senegal began in the 1860s and 1870s. The railway from Kayes was begun in 1881 and opened to Koulikoro in 1904, thus linking the upper limit of navigation on the Senegal to the navigable middle Niger. From then until 1960 this railway remained the main link with the sea and carried the major part of Mali's external trade. After the political break with Senegal in August of that year, the 'life-line' was closed for the first time in over fifty years* and Mali sought to develop an alternative route through Guinea. At present, the only practic- able alternative lies by trunk road and railway through Upper Volta and the Ivory Coast to Abidjan.

Mali is larger in area than Nigeria but has far less people (4.1 million in 1961). The southern part of the country is in the same latitude as northern Nigeria, while the north extends far into the Sahara. It is, therefore, a dry land, and agriculture without irrigation is only possible in parts of the south. Even in the extreme south of the country the rainy season is short. Because of this, together with high temperatures and rapid evaporation, Bamako's annual rainfall average of 44 inches is not

*It was re-opened on 22 June 1963 with better relations between Senegal and Mali.

very effective for agriculture, although it would be more than
enough in temperate latitudes.[1]

Both for communications and for production, the life of Mali
centres on the Niger valley, and it is here that most of the people
live.

The chain of lakes and water channels stretching southwards
from Timbuktu is all that now remains of the former inland
delta of the Niger and the lake into which it drained. Even
today, however, the river gradient is slight, and the consequent
annual floods have been used for centuries, both for crop
growing (millets) and for seasonal pasture. The area of lakes and
channels from Diafarabé to Timbuktu is known as the live
delta; the stretch from Sansanding to Diafarabé, the dead delta.

Irrigation in both parts of the delta was extended by the
French. In the live delta, work has been undertaken on a
generally small scale under the Department of Agriculture. The
dead delta has been the area of operations for one of Africa's
most ambitious irrigation schemes, the Niger Office project.

The Niger Office, a state organization, was set up in 1932, and
its main engineering work has been the construction of a dam at
Sansanding, begun in 1934 and finished in 1941. Its effect has
been to raise the river level some fourteen feet, with the aim of
making 'live' again the dried-up water channels from former
years.

Into this hitherto unproductive region African colonists have
been brought from other parts of Mali and from Upper Volta,
to be organized into cooperatives called Native Agricultural
Associations. These are financed partly by the Office, partly by
the members, and act both as providers of credit and as marketing agencies. Every colonist must observe certain cultivation
requirements, but after paying annual dues and contributing
towards the food and seed reserves of the Association, each
member may sell either through the cooperative or elsewhere.
In this way individualism and modern techniques are combined
with traditional attitudes towards communal life.[2]

Preceding and accompanying the development of this project
went years of research into soil, crops, and marketing organization. During the 1930s the whole region became 'a vast
agronomic laboratory',[3] including fruit orchards, a rice station,

a cotton research station, and an animal husbandry laboratory.

Grandiose in conception, the original project envisaged over 3 million irrigated acres employing about 800,000 colonists, and aimed to grow enough cotton to free France from American supplies. It has been in full operation since 1947, but by 1954 had been extended to include only 90,000 acres and some 24,000 colonists.[4]

The emphasis is now on rice rather than cotton, as this has been found more suitable for the poor soils and inexperienced farmers. Critics of the scheme argued that the expenditure of between £30 million and £40 million to irrigate 90,000 acres of rice fields was stupid, but this ignored the research work (always expensive) and the fact that the scheme is now on a sound technical and economic footing, with peasant farmers enjoying a standard of living some ten times higher than their neighbours.[5] In recent seasons the total value of crops grown by settlers has averaged approximately £83 per person, while several households enjoy net incomes of over £250. If such incomes can be maintained or even bettered, the Office du Niger will have little need to worry over the ultimate success of its enterprise.[6]

Live delta irrigation has been improved and extended by the Department of Agriculture, using simple and inexpensive methods to modify the annual floods, to conserve available water supplies and to extend the cultivable area. Although cultivation methods are inferior to the Niger Office project, the cost is negligible and by 1954 the Department had irrigated more than three times the acreage of the more expensive scheme.[7]

These two methods of land improvement in Mali provide a further example of the dilemma facing agricultural improvers all over Africa today. The large scheme, expensive in capital and skilled manpower, is probably the best in the long term. On the other hand, the short-term simple improvements are likely to bring more immediate benefits to more people, at a time when the large scheme has hardly begun to show results.

With the help of both types of improvement, Mali has become a food-exporting country. It produces each year some 14,000 tons of rice surplus to its needs, about 6,000 tons coming from areas developed by the Department of Agriculture and about 8,000 tons from the Niger Office areas.[8] The former areas produce more rice, but more is used for the subsistence of a larger population. The same areas also produce large quantities of fish, and groundnuts are an increasingly important export crop.

TABLE II

Exports of Mali in 1960 (by value)

	per cent
Groundnuts	40.0
Fish	22.8
Cotton	8.5
Live animals	10.6
Rice	5.8
Other	12.3

Total value 3,500 million francs

Source: *U.N. Yearbook of International Trade Statistics, 1961,* p. 412.

Outside these main agricultural areas the wealth of the country is in cattle, sheep, and goats, thousands of which are exported annually to the Ivory Coast, Ghana, and Nigeria.

GUINEA is agriculturally the poorest of the three states, and has the smallest population (3 million in 1960). Until a few years ago its main exports consisted of bananas and citrus fruits from plantations on the Fouta Djallon, many of which were owned by non-Africans. Increasingly, however, it has been realized that Guinea's economic future is as an industrial rather than an agricultural country.

This is surprising at first sight, because varied relief has produced an unusual climatic variety, which in turn has provided possibilities for a varied agriculture. Rice and palm oil from the coastal swamps, fruit from the Fouta Djallon, and tea and coffee from other highland areas have all developed to some degree. All are hampered, however, by the quality of Guinean soils.* Guinea contains some of the world's most extensive deposits of laterite which, together with high and heavy rainfall and consequent washing away of top soil, make large areas almost useless for agriculture. If a land with similar soils existed in Europe, two thirds would be regarded as unsuit-

*This is also true of much of Liberia and Sierra Leone.

able for either arable or pastoral farming. It has been estimated that

about 60 per cent of the country ought not to be cultivated ... About 30 per cent could be used if proper cultivation and anti-erosion methods were employed. Only about 10 per cent, mostly situated on the east coast and in river valleys, is capable of being cultivated without particular precautions.[9]

Although Guinea could conceivably be made more than self-sufficient in food, it is in its resources of bauxite, iron, and hydro-electric power that the real wealth – and so the main hope for the future – of the country lies.

As long ago as 1912 bauxite was discovered on the Los islands, offshore from Conakry, the capital. This was in easily worked surface deposits, but no attempt was made to exploit them until 1949, when a French subsidiary of the Aluminium Laboratories of Canada began operations. The first shipment of ore left Guinea in 1952, and by 1955 annual production had risen to nearly half a million tons. Because the ore was not needed in France and was of a type not treated by any European plant, it was shipped to Canada for processing.

The Los island deposits are expected to be exhausted by about 1970, and in anticipation of this event the same company has invested over £30 million in far richer deposits at Boké, about 100 miles north-west of Conakry, with part of the investment earmarked for the building of a railway and an alumina plant.

More important still has been the discovery and working of yet richer deposits in the Fouta Djallon by an international consortium of companies known as F.R.I.A., whose alumina plant began production in 1960. The firm is financed largely by French, Swiss, and American capital, but the development of its full potential depends on the completion of a dam on the Konkouré river at Sonapité to provide cheap hydro-electric power. Now that transport facilities have been provided by F.R.I.A., it is likely that the Konkouré scheme will go forward in stages, as and when funds become available.

Iron ore is also worked near Conakry with capital provided from private Western sources. One third of the finance comes from the British Iron and Steel Corporation, and the major part of the output is used by the United Kingdom.

TABLE 12

Exports of Guinea in 1960 (by value)

	per cent
Alumina	16.0
Coffee	15.5
Diamonds	13.0
Bananas	8.5
Bauxite	8.0
Palm kernels	7.0
Pineapples	6.0
Iron ore	5.5
Other	20.5

Total value 13,603 million francs

Source: *U.N. Yearbook of International Trade Statistics 1961*, p. 288.

Guinea is poor and even less developed than some of her neighbours, but she possesses the same advantages in the situation of her exploitable minerals as Britain enjoyed in the early days of the industrial revolution. Like most British coalfields, the reserves are near the coast, and transport is accordingly cheap. Moreover, they are reserves which are attracting private investment capital in a way which countries without such mineral deposits cannot hope to do.

Guinea's chief problem now is to finance the less profitable side of her development plan – the dams, further transport facilities, agricultural improvements, and social services – the growth of which was stopped short by the sudden withdrawal of French capital in 1958.

Since independence there has been a considerable growth of trade with East Germany, Czechoslovakia, and the Soviet Union. Of particular interest is the loan agreement concluded with China in 1960. This provides for the loan of £9million over three years, completely free of interest and repayable in Guinean goods or currency over ten years from 1970 onwards. Among other things it stipulates that Chinese technicians sent to Guinea shall not live at a higher standard than local men doing the same job.

Chinese methods of rapid economic growth do seem to have an attraction for the leadership. In an interview in 1959, Sekou

Touré, President of Guinea, expressed himself determined to go ahead with the Konkouré scheme. 'We shall build it with our own hands if necessary,' he said, and cited developments in China as an example. His own aim is to develop Guinea as an industrial country based on cheap electric power, producing aluminium houses, boats for river navigation, aircraft, trains, and cars.[10]

The truth seems to be that Guinea is determined on an industrial future and that for scarce capital she will go wherever she can get it. If it is not forthcoming in sufficient quantities, she may have to resort to popular mobilization on the Chinese model.

GHANA is the richest country in tropical Africa. The income per head of its 6.6 million population is not far short of £70 a year, and though this is not very high by European standards, it is three times as high as the average income per head in some other African states. This is one reason why Ghana was able to achieve independence before her neighbours. Linked with this greater prosperity was an older and more developed educational system which had by the 1950s produced a potential administrative élite. One measure of this greater wealth, educational advance and political progress is given by figures of newspaper circulation. (See Table 13, p. 124).

Ghana consists of the former Gold Coast Colony (the 50-150 mile wide coastal strip), Ashanti (inland from the former colony and centred on Kumasi), the Northern Territories, and that part of the former German colony of Togoland which elected to join newly independent Ghana in a U.N.-sponsored plebiscite.

The Northern Territories are relatively poor and undeveloped, resembling the thinly populated Middle Belt of Nigeria, since Ghana does not extend far enough northwards to embrace areas similar to the more thickly populated and Moslem-dominated Northern Region of Nigeria. Only in the extreme north-eastern tip of the country are population densities as high as those in the south. The politically and economically important areas of Ghana are Ashanti and the former Colony.

As elsewhere in West Africa, foreign settlements remained coastal until the late nineteenth century. From 1874 onwards these settlements were administered by Britain as the Gold

TABLE 13

Daily Newspapers, Copies in Circulation per 1,000 of population

Daily Newspapers		Copies in circulation per 1,000 of population
South Africa	(1959)	61
Ghana	(1961)	32
Rhodesia	(1959)	32
Kenya	(1961)	14
Angola	(1961)	9
Nigeria	(1961)	8
Uganda	(1960)	8
Sierra Leone	(1961)	8
Zambia	(1959)	7
S.W. Africa	(1957)	6
Gambia	(1959)	5
Tanganyika	(1961)	4
Ivory Coast	(1961)	3
Zanzibar	(1961)	3
Moçambique	(1960)	3
Congo (ex-Belgian)	(1959)	2
Cameroun	(1961)	2
Liberia	(1961)	1
Chad	(1961)	0.3

Source: *U.N. Statistical Yearbook 1962*, pp. 649–50.

Coast Colony, but inland the Ashanti Confederation of native states continued to exert considerable military and political power. In a series of seven Ashanti wars (the last in 1900) this obstacle to British expansion was eliminated and the Asantehene exiled to the Seychelles, from which he did not return until 1924. But there was no destruction of the native administration, and Ashanti regional feeling and pride were able to flourish under the British system of delegating as much local administration as possible to the existing native authorities.

When constitutional discussions took place immediately prior to independence, most Ashanti leaders would have preferred a federal system such as was to be developed in Nigeria, but here there was no approximate balance between Ashanti and the Colony, as between south and north in Nigeria. The Colony contained the greater part of the population, possessed the higher educational standards, and had produced the dominant political leadership, a leadership moreover which had turned away from tribalism and regional loyalties towards the establishment not only of a strong Ghana, but an ultimately united Africa.

The main component of political opposition in Ghana at the time of independence was Ashanti separatism. Since then 'liberal' opposition has increased under the strong rule of Nkrumah's Convention People's Party, but the strength of Ashanti separatism has declined and the government seem to enjoy general support throughout the country.

The wealth of Ghana is heavily dependent on cocoa, of which it is the world's leading producer, and which accounts for over half of its exports. Most of this comes from southern Ashanti, where over one fifth of the working male population is growing cocoa.[11]

The tree, native to South America, was introduced to Ghana, where conditions proved to be ideal for its cultivation. It needs fairly good soils, dislikes too much rain as well as a pronounced dry season (60 inches of well-distributed rain is ideal) and must be provided with shade. It needs little labour in cultivation and was, therefore, capable of rapid adoption by African smallholders. In spite of the ravages of swollen shoot virus disease (12 million trees were cut out between 1946 and 1961) cocoa continues to be the chief cash crop, often at the expense of food crops which have to be supplemented by imports.

Cocoa provides most of Ghana's wealth, but minerals are also important, and their significance is likely to increase in the future. Like cocoa, production of all the major minerals is confined to southern Ashanti and the coastal regions, with the richest concentration in an area close to the Kumasi-Takoradi railway.

Gold, Diamonds, Timber, and Manganese are the present principal contributors to national income after cocoa, but the immense bauxite deposits west of Kumasi are likely to overtake these once the Volta River project is under way.

The completion of the Volta River project will not only help to raise Ghana's already relatively high living standards and diversify her economy, but will provide opportunities for population growth and economic development in a thinly peopled area at present devoted largely to subsistence agriculture.

TABLE 14

Ghana. Exports 1958 (by value)

	per cent
Cocoa	59.7
Timber	10.8
Gold	10.1
Diamonds	8.3
Manganese	8.3
Bauxite	.5
Palm Kernels	.3
Other	2.0

SOURCE: *Statesman's Yearbook 1961*, p. 298.

Notes on Chapter 6

1. Harrison Church, *West Africa*, p. 254.
2. V. Thompson and R. Adloff, *French West Africa*, 1960, p. 369.
3. ibid., p. 368.
4. Harrison Church, op. cit., p. 247.
5. Thompson and Adloff, op. cit., p. 370.
6. G. H. T. Kimble, *Tropical Africa*. Vol. I., p. 177.
7. Harrison Church, op. cit., p. 245.
8. ibid., p. 251.
9. ibid., p. 389.
10. Article by Edwin S. Morrisby, in the *Manchester Guardian*, 7 January 1959.
11. Harrison Church, op. cit., p. 399.
    See also E. A. Boateng, *Geography of Ghana*, Cambridge University Press, 1959.

7 Gambia, Sierra Leone, and Liberia

These small countries share with Ghana and Nigeria the use of English as their official language. Gambia was acquired by Britain (from 1817 onwards) in order to prevent French possession of an important navigable river, while both Liberia and Sierra Leone were founded as homes for freed slaves from the Americas.

GAMBIA

Gambia as a geographical absurdity has already been discussed.[1] Its very existence is one of the best examples of European folly in the political fragmentation of the continent. Varying between 13 and 30 miles wide and extending for nearly 300 miles along both banks of the navigable Gambia river, this British colony is almost entirely surrounded by the territory of Senegal.

The river is not only the reason for Gambia's existence but remains its life-line of communications. All of the population (less than 300,000 in 1961) live within striking distance of the river and are dependent on it for their links with the outside world.

Ninety per cent of the population are peasant farmers whose production for sale is almost entirely limited to groundnuts. In 1959 the value of groundnut exports amounted to nearly £2,500,000, while other exports brought in less than £500,000.[2]

Groundnuts, first exported in 1830, are grown on the lighter sandy soils away from the riverside swamps, especially in the middle river areas, while the riverside and coastal swamps, useless for groundnuts, are now being developed for rice cultivation. Rice has not yet replaced millets as the staple food, but it is already the preferred food of most Gambians and may well replace millets in the not too distant future. Rice acreages have increased rapidly in recent years, largely due to a government-sponsored attempt to make the colony self-sufficient in food.

One interesting feature of the economy is the annual migration into Gambia of between five and ten thousand 'strange farmers', who come from Portuguese Guinea, Senegal, and Mali to grow groundnuts. They are given land and houses by their hosts in return for labour service, and return to their homes after the harvest in November.

Gambia is the only remaining British colony in West Africa, largely because it does not appear to have a viable future on its own.* To the outside observer the only rational solution seems to lie in some sort of union with Senegal, but development in the colonial period has been entirely at variance with progress towards such a union. The lack of any communications between the two territories, the development of an artificial port at Dakar instead of the more suitable Bathurst, and different systems of colonial administration all combine to make union difficult. Moreover, Senegal is already independent, and Gambians may resist any suggestion that they should simply be incorporated into an existing state and so lose their identity.

The first step in bringing about closer cooperation between the two countries was completed in 1958 with the trans-Gambia road linking northern Senegal with Casamance. Built by the French government and maintained by the Gambia government, it may yet be a symbol of real association in the future.

SIERRA LEONE

Sierra Leone is a small, mountainous country, a little smaller than Scotland, which occupies a unique place in formerly British West Africa. It represents in practical terms the early stirrings of Europe's conscience over the evils of the slave trade, and was established at the end of the eighteenth century as a home for ex-slaves, most of whom had fought with Britain in the American Revolution and who were settled at Freetown in 1792.

During the nineteenth century the British used Freetown as their main naval base for the suppression of the slave trade, and

*It has now been agreed that Gambia will become independent in 1965.

the capture of slaving ships led to the settlement of more slaves in the colony, so that by 1833 over 34,000 freed slaves had been settled there.[3]

This colony was by no means the country we know today. The ex-slaves were settled in a small area of the peninsula – in and to the south of Freetown – which constituted the Colony proper, and was ruled directly by the British Government until independence. Most of the country, which was not settled by ex-slaves, was only taken over in 1898 as 'Protectorate' and ruled indirectly through the native chiefs.

The descendants of the ex-slaves, numbering some 120,000 today, are known as Creoles and have until recently had little contact with the peoples of the interior. The vast majority of the population live outside the Creole area in the Protectorate.[4]

Rivalry between Colony and Protectorate, between Christian and non-Christian, between Creole and non-Creole continues down to the present day, largely as a result of Creole exclusiveness and sense of superiority.

This sense of superiority stems from a variety of causes. The system of indirect rule through the Chiefs in the Protectorate, distinct from direct rule by the British government in the Colony, helped to maintain a barrier between the Creoles and the rest of the population, while the Creoles enjoyed superior educational facilities and even developed their own language.

Fourah Bay College – the oldest institution of higher education in West Africa – was founded in 1827 at Freetown, and students there have been awarded Durham University Degrees since 1876. Since the mid nineteenth century the Creoles of Freetown have had access to an education denied to most other West Africans for nearly 100 years. Already by 1859 the first Creole Doctor of Medicine had graduated from a British university, and ever since the Creoles have supplied a steady stream of educated and qualified men not only for their own country but also for other parts of English-speaking West Africa.

Their sense of superiority thus stems in part from the advantages they enjoyed in training and education. Not till 1927 did the first non-Creole qualify as a medical doctor – the country's first Prime Minister, Sir Milton Margai.

Creole exclusiveness has also been aided by the development

of Krio – a form of English with some Spanish, French, and Portuguese words. It has no written tradition because it is the language of a group educated in English, but it is preserved in folk-tales and proverbs and used as the language of social intercourse in the Creole community.

For the rest, the peoples of the Protectorates are composed of thirteen different tribes speaking as many different languages or dialects. There are, however, two major tribes – the Mende of the North and the Temne of the south – both with about 30 per cent of the total population.

Like other similar stations along the west coast, Sierra Leone proved a proverbial 'White Man's Grave'. Between 1814 and 1885 no less than five Governors and seven acting Governors died at their posts or on the way home, usually of malaria or yellow fever. As a result of advances in preventive medicine the country is no longer very unhealthy, but for much of the year the climate is uncomfortable, especially on the coast. Monthly mean temperatures at Freetown range from 78 to 82 degrees F. and in the rainy season, from June to September and beyond, there may be long periods of steady rain. Freetown has an annual rainfall of 118.7 inches.

The very high rainfall and the intensity of the rains lead to rapid run-off, severe leaching, and a high degree of lateritization. Coupled with this there is a density of population – unusual in this part of West Africa – which has in turn led to the removal of some 95 per cent of the original forest cover.[5]

In the subsistence economy rice, especially upland rice, is the main food crop. Only in parts of the north-east is the country dry enough for millets, while in the north-west and centre cassava replaces rice. These inland areas suffer in extreme from all the hazards, both natural and man-made, to which agriculture is subjected in tropical Africa; leaching, lateritization, soil erosion, and bad farming practices have seriously reduced their potential. It is in the coastal swamps, therefore, some 20 miles in width, that the future of Sierra Leone's agriculture would seem most profitably to lie.

Mangroves are being cut and swamps being cleared to make way for the growth of swamp rice. Over the last seventy years some 80,000 acres have been developed. Swamp clearance is hard and expensive, but once it is completed the work of cultivation is comparatively easy.

TABLE 15

Sierra Leone: Food Crop Acreages

Upland rice	570,000
Swamp rice	80,000
Millets and sorghums	30,000
Maize	25,000
Cassava	46,000

SOURCE: Colonial Office *Annual Report 1959.*

There is no doubt that further increases in swamp rice acreages would help to halt soil degradation in the interior by reducing the cultivation of upland rice and would eventually enable the country to become a rice exporter. In recent years, however, rice has had to be imported owing to a diversion of labour from farming to the more profitable digging for diamonds.

The major agricultural export at the moment is oil palm kernels, mostly from semi-wild trees in the vicinity of Freetown. Other agricultural exports are kola nuts, coffee, cocoa, and ginger, but these make only a small contribution to the national income.

In the last ten years the economic future of Sierra Leone has changed dramatically with the rapid increase in the production and export of iron ore and of diamonds.

TABLE 16

Sierra Leone: Exports 1961 (by value)

	per cent
Diamonds (from 35% in 1959)	63.0
Iron ore	18.5
Palm kernels	9.7
Coffee	2.4
Cocoa	1.8
Other	4.6

Total value £25 million

SOURCE: *U. N. Yearbook of International Trade Statistics 1961*, p. 556.

This upsurge in mineral production has placed the economy of the country on a much firmer base than before. As a purely agricultural land it would hardly have had the resources to attempt tackling the challenge of independence with any hope of success. Now it can look forward to the development of an economy which already possesses some degree of diversification.

There has been considerable controversy over the mining of diamonds. Some ten years ago it was discovered that diamonds could be picked up quite easily in the river beds – and therefore marketed illegally in defiance of a monopoly granted to a private corporation. Police were unable to control the thousands of illegal miners who entered the diamondiferous areas in search of this new source of wealth, so that the corporation's monopoly had to be terminated and the private diggers allowed to mine under government licence. The government was initially alarmed at the illegal mining, as it suffered considerable losses of revenue. The outcome has, however, proved satisfactory in several different ways. Wealth has been spread more widely in a country which is still very poor; people have been encouraged to move away from their villages and prosper elsewhere; and it has reduced the grip of foreign capital on the country's economic life.[6]

Iron ore production has nearly doubled over the last ten years in response to private foreign investment. Further development in this and other fields is likely to be hampered, however, by poor and difficult communications. The 2 ft 6 ins. gauge railway has served a useful purpose, especially for the oil palm districts, but road development only really started after the Second World War. It took till 1950 before the road into neighbouring Guinea was completed.

Politically, the government of the ruling People's Party seems more likely to follow the lead of Nigeria than of Ghana. A comparatively diverse economy and access to overseas investment in the mines gives Sierra Leone a certain stability.

LIBERIA

Liberia was like Sierra Leone in being founded by philanthropists as a home for ex-slaves, though the organization concerned there was the American Colonization Society. The first party of freed slaves was landed in 1822, and from then onwards the colony received a steady stream of immigrants, especially slaves freed by the American Navy. Liberia differed from Sierra Leone, however, in gaining its independence as early as 1847.

Lacking either techniques or capital, and landed on an inhospitable coast, the freed slaves never had a chance to do more than merely survive in stagnation and chronic indebtedness. Their state became a symbol to which those seeking to prove Negro inferiority could point. Up to 1939 Monrovia had no telephone system, piped water, or sewage disposal; there were no railways, roads, or ports; and the government was notorious for its corruption and despotism.

There is the same division as in Sierra Leone between the descendants of returned slaves (the Americo-Liberians*) and the vast majority of the inhabitants, except that the Americo-Liberians have not enjoyed the educational opportunities of the Creoles of Sierra Leone. Even as late as 1948 there was not one indigenous medical practitioner in Liberia. Until after the Second World War, the rule of the Americo-Liberians over the rest of the population was absolute. The first independent Negro republic in tropical Africa had a native policy no different from that of a colonial power, with district commissioners operating under a system of indirect rule.

The Americo-Liberians came to spend more and more time playing a closed game of politics and pursuing an elaborate social life which was modelled on that of the white plantation aristocracy in the American South. For over a century a wide gulf continued to exist between them and the vast majority of the population in the hinterland, a population which remained one of the most primitive and isolated in the whole of Africa. The master-slave pattern which they had known in the American South was transported by the Americo-Liberians to Africa. They were the masters; the native population, the slaves.

For years a small group of men 'played musical chairs with the available government offices'.[7] There were no skilled

*About 20,000 of the 1,290,000 people in the country are Americo-Liberians.

workers, and the only cash income received by any Liberians went to the politicians.

By the 1930s the country had sunk so low that an international commission judged it guilty of procuring forced labour from among its own native population. Labourers were being shipped with the connivance of government officials from Liberia to French Gabon and Fernando Po, under conditions scarcely distinguishable from slave trading.

The modern development of Liberia stems from the beginnings of the Firestone Rubber Company's operations in 1926. Since then Liberia has been developed (and largely controlled) by a few large American firms, though since the end of the Second World War U.S. government investment has also played an important part in development.

Firestone has two estates, a large one near Monrovia and a small one near Harper. Since the first trickle of exports in 1933, production has grown in size and value until today rubber still forms nearly one half of Liberia's total export trade, despite subsequent diversification of the economy.

TABLE 17

Liberia: Exports 1959 (by value)

	per cent
Rubber	45.9
Iron ore	42.2
Palm kernels	3.4
Diamonds	3.2
Other	5.3

Total value £23 million

SOURCE: *Statesman's Year Book 1961*, p. 1216.

In spite of its dominant position in the economy, Firestone employs less than 30,000 people. Its operations, indeed, provide a perfect example of Africa's highly developed economic islands in the midst of a stagnant subsistence economy. The plantations themselves are very efficient, giving the highest yields per acre of any rubber estates in the world.

In addition to profitably growing rubber, Firestone has

established all the modern civic amenities in the vicinity of its estates, and has branched out into other fields of manufacturing activity. Medical, health, and educational services, roads, a hydro-electric plant, a radio station, and factories producing rubber products are examples of the company's activities and interests. In 1955 nearly 40 per cent of government revenue came from Firestone.

Since 1945 the American government itself has taken a direct interest in Liberia's development, starting with the construction between 1945 and 1948 of a huge new deep-water harbour at Monrovia, which cost $20 million. Between 1950 and 1958, U.S. government loans and grants to Liberia amounted to over $10 million, and have been used for economic surveys, the development of agriculture, and the beginning of a network of communications and other essential public services.[8]

Other large companies besides Firestone have also taken a hand. The Liberia Company has interested itself in plantation agriculture and communications, while the Liberia Mining Company has added a new and important commodity to Liberia's list of exports. High-grade iron ore some 45 miles north-west of Monrovia in the Bomi hills is now being successfully worked, following the completion of the mineral railway in 1951. Exports are now running at over 2 million tons a year, and it is estimated that there are deposits of 40 million tons of high-grade and 200 million tons of lesser-grade ore still to be worked. There is an even larger deposit of iron in the eastern province, which is being developed by a joint Swedish-U.S. company.

Another of Liberia's booming activities in recent years has been the growth of her merchant fleet. With Panama, she provides for the world's shipping one of the best-used flags of convenience, which gives owners the advantages of low registration fees and taxation with little control over their ships. Between 1954 and 1959 the total tonnage of Liberian-registered ships rose from 1.22 million tons to over 11 million tons.

From sad and dismal beginnings Liberia has made substantial strides during the last twenty years, both in economic development and in the reform of her government and administration. There is still very heavy reliance on a few large American companies, of course, and the U.S. still takes some 90 per cent of Liberia's exports. Yet Liberia has begun to take a respectable place in the community of independent African states, and the sneers of only thirty years ago are a great deal less justified.

Notes on Chapter 7

1. See Chapter 3 above.
2. Colonial Office Report, *Gambia* 1958 *and* 1959, p. 7.
3. R. J. Harrison Church, *West Africa*, p. 301. For a detailed account see R. R. Kuczynski, *Demographic Survey of the British Colonial Empire, Vol.* I, *West Africa*, 1948, Chapter 2.
4. 1948 *Population Figures.*
    Colony 124,657.
    Protectorate 1,858, 275.
5. F. J. Martin, *A Preliminary Survey of the Vegetation of Sierra Leone*, 1938, quoted in Harrison Church, op. cit., p. 304.
6. C. Fyfe, 'A Peaceful Achievement in Africa', article in the *Listener*, 27 April 1961, p. 726.
7. W. A. Hance, *African Economic Development*, pp. 235–6.
8. ibid., p. 226.
    See also:
    H. R. Jarret, *A Geography of Sierra Leone and Gambia*, 1954.
    C.O.I. *Sierra Leone: the Making of a Nation*, 1950.
    C.O.I. *Sierra Leone*, 1961.
    R. Lewis, *Sierra Leone*, 1954 (Corona Library).
    A. T. Porter, *Creoledom*, 1963.

8 French-speaking Africa and Portuguese Guinea

The rapidity with which political independence has come to the former French colonies is spectacular even by African standards. It represents a dramatic reversal of traditional French policy towards her dependencies, out of which have emerged fourteen different independent states. Twelve of these fourteen were incorporated in the former French West Africa and French Equatorial Africa, while the former German colonies of Togo and Cameroun were held under U.N. Trusteeship.

As early as 1848 France had granted full citizenship rights to the people of the Senegalese coastal towns, but throughout the rest of Black Africa the policy pursued was one of permanent close association with France rather than complete assimilation. Ultimately full assimilation might come, but only after the completion of France's civilizing mission – a mission which would be completed only when all of Black Africa was fully French in language and culture.

In pursuance of this policy, administration was increasingly conducted through a French-educated African élite, and the traditional chiefs were either replaced or their powers allowed to lapse. The French-speaking educated African had more political power and therefore less political grievances than his English-speaking counterpart. African politicians sat in France's Parliament, became cabinet ministers, and generally participated in the political life of the metropolitan country in a way which would have been unthinkable in Britain. These French Africans were frequently said to be more French than the French; and there were many who thought it unlikely that such men would wish to take their peoples to full independence from France.

The group which led the breakaway movement was the Guinean Democratic Party of Sekou Touré. Under the terms of the French referendum in 1958 General de Gaulle offered the overseas territories of France a choice between full internal autonomy, within a new French Community, or immediate independence. In the event, Guinea opted for immediate independence and the rest for internal autonomy.

Guinea represented in 1958 the extreme nationalist wing in French African politics. 'It will fall to us,' said Sekou Touré, 'to preserve, for Guinea and for Africa, the honour of African Man.... We shall vote "No" to a community which is merely the French Union re-christened ... We shall vote "No" to inequality.'[1]

Guinea stood alone in 1958. French aid was stopped, experts withdrawn, and trade agreements terminated. But it proved impossible to isolate the rest of French Africa from the rush to independence which Ghana and Guinea had started. There were those like Mali and Senegal which wanted collective independence for the whole of French West Africa. There were those like the Ivory Coast which wanted neither complete independence nor federation. One and all, however, with varying degrees of enthusiasm, found it expedient to follow the lead of Guinea and Ghana, and all are now independent sovereign states. After Guinea, there was no complete break between France and its other former colonies. Even Mali continues to receive French economic aid and technical assistance.

It has already been shown that the level of French investment in her overseas territories since 1948 was considerably higher than Britain's in English-speaking Africa.[2] It should be said, of course, that this was more than ever necessary because the level of pre-war investment had been so abysmally low – much lower than in the British colonies which were, as a result, economically more advanced. This new high rate of investment has been maintained and indeed even increased since the attainment of independence, but it has been coupled with a policy of inter-territorial economic planning for the whole area and much closer economic ties with France than the ex-British colonies have with Britain. With the exception of Guinea, the ex-French territories do about 70 per cent of their trade with France.[3]

As in the rest of the continent, development has been very uneven; countries with a favourable coastal situation have been able to advance much farther and much faster than the inland states. In 1956, Senegal accounted for 35 per cent and the Ivory Coast for 44 per cent of the total exports of French West Africa. And this imbalance has been maintained in the era of overall economic planning. In the west, Senegal and the Ivory Coast have received much the largest share of the total funds available, partly no doubt because so much investment has gone into port and communications development to serve the whole area. Similarly the Congo Republic has been developed as the main hub of communications for the whole equatorial region.

TABLE 18

French Government Investment in Tropical Africa 1947–57

	£ million
Senegal	46.8
Ivory Coast	36.3
Congo	30.3
Mali	26.4
Guinea	26.2
Chad	18.6
Central African Republic	16.8
Dahomey	16.6
Gabon	16.5
Upper Volta	14.5
Niger	8.4
Mauritania	5.0

SOURCE: *French Economic Assistance in West and Equatorial Africa: A Decade of Progress 1948–58* (French Government Publication).

STATES OF THE SAVANNA ZONE

SENEGAL

Senegal, with its coastal situation and consequent control over inland lines of communication, rivals the Ivory Coast for the leadership of French-speaking Africa, but the reasons for its supremacy over many of its neighbours lie in its strategic situation and political experience rather than in any inherent economic strength.

The port of Dakar was developed from 1898 as a naval base

and subsequently became a great centre of air communications and an important port of call on both South American and African shipping routes. Indeed, it was developed by the French to be the administrative centre for the whole of French West Africa. As a result there have come to this city of over 250,000 inhabitants many of the abler and more ambitious people from the surrounding areas. Its favourable climate has attracted over 30,000 European residents[4] and it already has an established industry in soap, textile, canning, oil refining, and other products. Dakar without the rest of French West Africa is, however, rather like Vienna without the Austro-Hungarian Empire – a capital without a country – for the rest of Senegal is, like Gambia, heavily dependent on groundnut production.

About 40 per cent of the cultivated area is devoted to groundnuts, and most of the rest of the staple food – millets. Groundnut exports date back to the 1840s, encouraged by the needs of French soap manufacturers, and were given an opportunity to grow by subsequent railway development. Unlike the production of neighbouring Gambia, many of the nuts are processed in local refineries.*

Efforts to diversify the economy include the Senegal Delta irrigation scheme, under which over 13,000 acres have, since 1948, been irrigated for swamp rice cultivation. This has not, however, been a financial success so far.

Senegal has been heavily dependent on the usefulness of Dakar. Its future would seem equally dependent on the goodwill of neighbouring states, including Mali, with whom relations were broken in 1960 and only recently repaired.

MAURITANIA

Mauritania is, in population, the smallest of the states in ex-French West Africa, with less than a million people, most of them nomadic. The country is largely desert† and its very existence has been challenged by Morocco, which claims the whole

---

*Of total exports in 1961, 38 per cent of 30,657 million francs were groundnut oil, 37 per cent groundnuts, and 7.7 per cent were oil-seed cake and meal. (*U.N. Yearbook*, op. cit., p. 551.)

†Total exports in 1961 were only 535 million francs, of which over half was fish. (*U.N. Yearbook*, op. cit., p. 417.)

of the territory as its own. Possession of Mauritania by Morocco would, of course, provide a continuous geographical link with her southern allies. This challenge to Mauritania's existence has embittered relations between Morocco and the French-speaking states of Black Africa, for these last are very jealous of their territorial integrity, however colonial the genesis of their frontiers.

Interest has quickened in this barren desert country with the discovery in 1952 of valuable iron ore deposits in the Kedia d'Idjil hills in the far north-west, inland from Spanish Sahara. Prospecting has gone on ever since and a mining camp has been constructed with good water available from local wells. Eventually it is estimated that a town of over 6,000 people will exist there, with several million tons of ore being exported each year.

As so often in Africa, the overriding problem is transport. The nearest port, in Spanish territory, is not particularly good. Port Etienne is better and belongs to Mauritania – but railway construction will be more costly. A line is at present being built entirely in Mauritania, which will include an expensive tunnel designed to avoid some eight miles of Spanish territory.[5]

Surprisingly enough, one of the largest sources of future income may be tourism. Port Etienne has pleasant beaches and a temperature from November to May which ranges between 54 and 84 degrees F. In the ever widening search for a quiet and sure escape from the European winter, Mauritania may come to rank with currently more fashionable refuges.

UPPER VOLTA

Upper Volta lies in one of the most densely populated parts of the west African savanna zone. Its population of 3½ million is greater than that of the Ivory Coast in a rather smaller area, but its density bears little relation to the richness of its natural resources or the development of its economy. It is a poor and infertile land, almost entirely devoted to agriculture, with a degree of over-population unusual in this part of Africa. The reasons seem to lie in a long period of political stability and successful Mossi* resistance to the Fulani invasions of the nineteenth century.

*The chief tribe of the country.

Over-population and underdevelopment have led to a considerable migration of workers into neighbouring countries. Some have gone to Mali as colonists in the Niger Office scheme, some to work in the mines and on the cocoa farms of Ghana.

Economic ties with Ghana are close, but Upper Volta is associated with the Ivory Coast, Niger, and Dahomey in the loose partnership of the Conseil de l'Entente. In an effort to encourage closer economic association within the Conseil and promote development, the railway from the Ivory Coast was extended to the capital, Ouagadougou, but much of Upper Volta's trade still goes through Ghana. The most valuable export indeed, is cattle, most of which is driven live into Ghana.*

NIGER

Niger is slightly smaller in area than Mali but larger than Nigeria, with only some 2½ million people. Of these the Hausa constitute the biggest group (¾ million), and Niger thus has close cultural as well as geographical links with Northern Nigeria, links made stronger by the fact that Niger's line of communications with the outside world lies through Kano.

The population is concentrated in the south-west along the Niger river, and the main export crop is groundnuts.† Niger is drier than Mali, and there are accordingly fewer cattle for export. The cattle trade is, like the export of groundnuts, directed through Kano. Niger is one of the most remote of the African states and its biggest immediate economic problem is the development of adequate communications with the outside world. To this end the great bulk of French investment in the last ten years has gone into road building.

---

*Total exports in 1961 were only 812 million francs, of which 64 per cent was live animals and 12 per cent oil seeds and nuts. (*U.N. Yearbook*, op. cit., p. 47.)

†Fifty-eight per cent of a total value of 3,108 million francs. A further 13.5 per cent is accounted for by live cattle. (1960 figures, *U.N. Yearbook*, op. cit., p. 473.)

STATES OF THE WEST AFRICAN COAST

IVORY COAST

Ivory Coast ranks with Senegal as one of the two richest components of former French West Africa. In addition, under the formidable leadership of M. Houphouët-Boigny, it has played a leading role in seeking to maintain close economic and political ties with France.

Economic development has until recently been hampered by lack of a suitable port, as Abidjan was cut off from the sea by a persistent sand bar. Only in 1950 were the engineering problems overcome, the Vridi canal opened, and Abidjan able to be developed as a major trade outlet.

The economy is based almost entirely on agriculture and the processing of agricultural products, although there is a small diamond mining industry.

TABLE 19

Ivory Coast. Exports 1961 (by value)

	per cent
Coffee	46.6
Cocoa	22.5
Wood	19.0
Other	11.9
Total value 43,603 million francs	

SOURCE: *U.N. Yearbook of International Trade Statistics 1961*, p. 364.

Unusually for west Africa, about a quarter of the coffee crop is produced on European-owned plantations; but cocoa, introduced from the Gold Coast, is nearly all produced by African smallholders.

TOGO

Togo is the smallest independent state in Africa, consisting of that part of former German Togoland which became a French mandated territory in 1919. The part allotted to Britain elected to join independent Ghana. Togo is an entirely agricultural country, and 55 per cent of all exports consist of cocoa and coffee, with subsidiary palm kernels and copra.

Remarkably, among the former subjects of France, many people in Togo are literate in an African language and not in French. This is particularly true of the Ewe, for whom the Germans soon worked out an orthography and started to teach it. Like Swahili in Tanganyika, this has been an important factor in the development of nationalism, and may be measured particularly in the concern of the Ewe to be united with their fellow Ewe across the border in Ghana.

Togo is also remarkable in that it also has an English press which comes in from Ghana. There has been much population movement and commerce across the border, and many Ewe can speak and read English as well as (or instead of) French.[6]

It was thought at one time that the Ewe leaders of Togo would wish to join with Ghana,[7] but an independent existence has proved more attractive to them.

DAHOMEY

Dahomey has close affinities with neighbouring Nigeria. Just as the Ewe are divided between Togo and Ghana, so the Yoruba-speaking people spill over from Nigeria into Dahomey.

Like the Mossi of Upper Volta, Dahomey had a powerful native political organization prior to French occupation. One

TABLE 20

Dahomey: Exports 1959 (by value)

	per cent
Palm kernels	37
Groundnuts	15
Palm oil	14
Coffee	7
Fish	6
Other	21

SOURCE: *Yearbook of International Trade Statistics 1959*, Vol. I., p. 207.

consequence of this is that there has been considerable development of African-owned plantation agriculture, a system established in the mid nineteenth century by the labour of prisoners.

At present Dahomey is an entirely agricultural country, but deposits exist of high-grade iron ore and chromite.

CAMEROUN

Cameroun, like Togo, was divided in 1919 between French and British administered mandates. By a plebiscite held in 1961, most of the former British area (i.e. the Southern Cameroons) elected to re-join with independent Cameroun rather than with Nigeria. The Northern British Cameroons elected to join Nigeria.

The population is concentrated in two main areas. The first, in the far north, south of Lake Chad, corresponds in population and economic activities with Northern Nigeria; the second, in the south-west, is where the main wealth of the country lies.

With an income per head of over $100 per annum, Cameroun must be counted as one of the richest countries in tropical Africa. Largely this is due to the German development of plantation agriculture in the fertile highland areas of the south-west, a development which was continued under subsequent administrations. The plantations are mainly African-owned and the chief export crops are cocoa, palm kernels, bananas, coffee and cotton.

TABLE 21

Exports of Cameroun in 1961 (by value)

	per cent
Cocoa and cocoa butter	29.0
Coffee	21.0
Alumina	19.8
Wood	6.7
Cotton	6.0
Bananas	3.4
Oil seeds and nuts	3.0
Other	11.1

Total value 24, 197 million francs

SOURCE: *U.N. Yearbook of International Trade Statistics 1961*, p. 123.

THE EQUATORIAL STATES

The Equatorial States – Central African Republic, Chad, Gabon, and Congo (ex-French) – are among the most backward, thinly populated, and underdeveloped regions in the whole of Africa, though a great deal has been done in the years since the Second World War.

CHAD

Chad is the most remote of all the former French colonies. Not only are its communications with the outside world poor, but there is no good system of internal communications in the territory. Few roads exist and these are of poor quality. The northern half of the territory is desert, and in the central areas the land is too dry for anything except extensive cattle farming. Only in the south-west is there enough rainfall for crops, and here cotton has been developed as a cash crop.* Increased production of cotton and meat, with reduced transport costs for their export, are the main lines of development likely to be followed in the future.

The whole area has been hampered by lack of good communications. The coastal rain-forest prevented the early development of transport links with the more populous interior, while the generally low density of population (less than five per square mile) makes modern roads and railways extremely costly undertakings.

Potentially the richest area is the savanna zone of the CENTRAL AFRICAN REPUBLIC, where cotton growing and cattle ranching have been started.

GABON

It is Gabon, however, which has the best immediate prospect of income for future development. Gabon, the land of Schweitzer's 'Primeval Forest', has recently started to export both oil and

*Of total exports worth 4,519 million francs, 93 per cent were cotton (1961 figures, *U.N. Yearbook*, op. cit., p. 148).

uranium with the aid of Franco-American investment.* This is probably the main reason why the country has stood aloof from the close economic and administrative union which the Equatorial states enjoyed under French rule.

Much of French investment in the area has concentrated on the improvement of communications, especially the expansion of port facilities at Brazzaville and Pointe Noire and the construction of the rail link between them. This accounts for the very high rate of post-war investment in the CONGO REPUBLIC as compared with its neighbours. Brazzaville, like Dakar in the West, was designed to be both the administrative capital and the economic hub of the whole of Equatorial Africa. With the coming of independence, Congo, like Senegal, will be heavily dependent on the cooperation and goodwill of its neighbours.

The continuing close relationship between France and most of her former colonies has had two important results, one political and the other economic. Politically, although France has lost an empire, she has gained ten or eleven independent allies.[8] In an age where votes in the U.N. General Assembly are important in international affairs, the support of the French African states† has, on occasions, been of immense importance to France. They have, for example, succeeded in modifying U.N. General Assembly resolutions over Algeria and enabled France to continue until 1962 to postpone a settlement.

The economic result of continuing close association is possibly longer-lasting. When France joined the European Common Market she took her African territories with her. This means that when the market becomes fully effective, the exports of French Africa will have duty-free entry into the whole Common Market area, but that other African exports will not. Cocoa from the Ivory Coast, for example, will have a tariff advantage over cocoa from Ghana. If Britain entered the Common Market without negotiating similar privileges for Commonwealth countries, it would have to admit French African products duty free,

*Of total exports in 1961 worth 13,530 million francs, 69 per cent were wood, 16 per cent petroleum, and 9 per cent uranium (*U.N. Yearbook*, op. cit., pp. 245–6).

†Former French West Africa, French Equatorial Africa, and Madagascar (excluding Guinea and Mali).

while imposing tariffs on goods from Ghana, Nigeria, and the other Commonwealth countries. As they stand at present, the Common Market arrangements in Africa serve to perpetuate economic and political divisions between the French- and English-speaking areas.[9]

The remaining political fragments of west Africa belong to Spain and Portugal.

The Spanish possessions in Africa are the least significant of the European colonies. *Spanish Sahara* is virtually uninhabited with only 13,000 people, but will one day no doubt provide material for active dispute between Spain and the two rival claimants Morocco and Mauritania. *Spanish Guinea*, sandwiched between Cameroun and Gabon, is hardly more important with just over 150,000 people. It is likely to remain an anachronistic foreign enclave long after the independence of the rest of the continent.

More important to Spain are the volcanic islands of FERNANDO PO and ANNOBON which, like their Portuguese counterparts, have had their fertile soils developed for plantation agriculture, developed from the turn of the century with cocoa as the main crop, together with some coffee and palm kernels. Like São Tomé, Fernando Po imports migrant labour on a contract basis.

PORTUGUESE GUINEA

Portuguese Guinea is Portugal's remaining foothold in west Africa. Set between the Senegalese province of Casamance and independent Guinea, it is the third-smallest political unit in west Africa, with only about half a million people.

Unlike the other Portuguese territories, it is not a country of extensive white settlement[10] or of plantation agriculture. As with its southern neighbour, many of the coastal mangrove swamps have been cleared for rice cultivation: like that of its northern neighbour, its main export crop is groundnuts. Together with palm products, these make up about 80 per cent by value of the colony's exports.

Notes on Chapter 8

1. Speech to Territorial Conference of P.G.D., 14 September 1958 in Conakry. Quoted by T. Hodgkin and R. Schachter in 'French-speaking West Africa in Transition', special issue of *International Conciliation*, May 1960, p. 420.
2. See Chapter 5 above.
3. Much of Guinea's trade has been switched to Eastern Europe, which in 1959 took 16 per cent of exports and sent 9 per cent of imports.
   (Hodgkin and Schachter, op. cit., p. 423.)
4. Climatically it is far superior to Bathurst in Gambia.
5. G. Harrison Church, 'Problems and Development of the Dry Zone of West Africa', in *Geographical Journal*, June 1961.
6. Committee on Inter-African Relations, *Report on the Press in West Africa*, 1961, p. 24.
   (Mimeographed. Distributed by Dept. of Extra-Mural Studies, University College, Ibadan, Nigeria.)
7. See Chapter 3 above.
8. *U.N. Review*, February 1961, p. 45.
   The eleven did not include Togo, which has been less pro-French than the others on a number of occasions.
9. See also Aaron Segal, 'Africa Newly Divided', in *Journal of Modern African Studies*, March 1964, p. 73.
10. 1950 Population 508,970 of which

Balante	160,296 (the coastal people)
Fulani	108,402
Manjalus	71,712
Mandingo	53,750
Whites	2,263

Source: Texeiria da Mota, *Guiné Portuguesa*, 1954.

Central Africa
9 Angola, Moçambique, São Tomé, and the ex-Belgian Congo

Portugal was the first European country to colonize in Africa; Belgium, one of the last. Both have ruled over enormous territories and both have ruled with a paternalistic attitude to their subjects. They have allowed no political opposition to develop and no political leaders to mature. Both have attracted world attention only in the last few years. There were, however, significant differences in the policies and programmes of the two countries.

The Belgians in the Congo, while intending to stay as rulers for a long time to come, started on a long-term programme leading to eventual self-government and undertook an ambitious ten-year development plan, financed largely by the mining industries of Katanga and Kasai. The Portuguese, on the other hand, have only been actively developing the interior of either Angola or Moçambique for the last twenty years, and they still regard all their overseas possessions as integral parts of the mother country. Portuguese policy is in theory fully assimilationist; that is, all the inhabitants of their territories are entitled to the full rights of citizenship once they have achieved the required standard of 'civilization'. Very few Africans have, however, acquired this status of *assimilado*.

In the early 1930s the Salazar regime began to revive the consciousness of Portugal's imperial destiny as intrinsic to its programme of national regeneration, a revival stirred by such phrases as 'the magnificent certainty that we are the third colonial power in the world'.[1] In this new consciousness of empire, the territory which has loomed largest in the minds of both politicians and economic planners is the relatively unknown land of Angola. Some four times the size of the United Kingdom, Angola is the promised land of the Portuguese Empire.

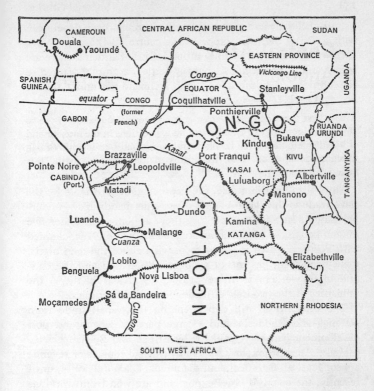

MAP 19. The Congo and Angola

ANGOLA

The coastal strip (up to 100 miles wide) is kept both arid and cool for the latitude by the cold Benguela ocean current, which flows along the coast. Even Luanda, only 600 miles from the equator, has only eleven inches of rain a year. Inland, however, the land rises sharply, and the rainfall increases. It is the interior plateaux which constitute the focus of current development plans. The north, between Malange and the Congo border, has a tropical climate and plantation agriculture has been developed, with coffee as the main crop. In the centre (Bié) around Nova Lisboa and the south (Huila) around Sá da Bandeira, there are higher and cooler regions, sparsely settled, admirably suited to agricultural development, and with a climate not unlike that of Portugal itself.[2]

The first three centuries of Angola's history, from about 1550 to 1850, is a chronology of small wars and expeditions in the interior and of a dedicated commerce in black humanity, most of it with Brazil, which made up more than four fifths of total exports during this period.[3]

More than anything else, the depopulation of Angola by the slave trade is the cause of one of its chief handicaps – under-population. In this vast territory there are only just under five million people, of whom some 200,000 are white. This, coupled with Portugal's own inability to provide either the men or the money required, has meant economic stagnation and the emigration of workers to more prosperous areas, chiefly to the industries of the (ex-Belgian) Congo and the Rhodesias.

The economy is still dependent on the transit trade from Katanga and Rhodesia, and a large part of railway and port development had been paid for by British and Belgian private capital.* Apart from this, Angola's principal sources of revenue are coffee, sisal, fish meal, and diamonds. Diamonds were, until recently, the colony's chief export and are won from workings near the Congo border across which lies the much bigger diamond field of Kasai. Mining is controlled by the Diamond Company of Angola (Diamang). Tucked away in this remote corner of the country with its headquarters in a garden city of its own creation (Dundo), Diamang is a colony within a colony and very much its own master.

The fishing industry and the processing of fish meal, much of which goes to the United States, are both centred on Benguela and Moçamedes, towns far more reminiscent of Portugal than of Africa. In 1955 oil was discovered near Luanda, and this has given promise of an economic future.

*The biggest shareholder in the Benguela railway is the British Company, Tanganyika Concessions. With political disorders in the Congo, much more copper traffic fell to this railway in 1961 than in previous years.

TABLE 22

Exports of Angola, 1961

	Percentage by value
Coffee	36.0
Diamonds	18.0
Sisal	8.1
Fish and fish meal	7.1
Other (Mainly cotton, wood, palm oil, sugar)	33.8

Total Value 3,874 million escudos

SOURCE: *U.N. Yearbook of International Trade Statistics 1961*, p. 49.

White Settlement in Angola

The central and southern highlands are the scene of an experiment unparalleled in Africa today – the settlement of Portuguese families as smallholders working their own land and tending their own cattle without the help of native labour.

Deliberate encouragement of white settlement did not start until the 1940s, when it was decided officially for the first time that 'the rich extensive colonial lands, undeveloped and sparsely populated, are the natural complement for metropolitan agriculture. . . . In addition they will take care of that part of the metropolis's excessive population which Brazil does not wish to accept'.[4] A further reason is the drive to demonstrate to Africans, by example, the Portuguese way of life.

Early efforts at planned colonization on the Huila plateau were not very successful, but in 1952 began the first of a series of planned colonization projects known as *colonatos*. The site of the first pilot scheme was at Cela on the Amboin plateau, about 240 miles north-west of Nova Lisboa. Here by 1954 over 200 Portuguese families had been installed, each receiving a house, seeds, livestock, and over 100 acres of land. A conscious effort was made to re-create the atmosphere of rural Portugal, and wherever possible immigrants were chosen from the same home district.

The white population of Angola grew from 44,000 in 1940 to 110,000 in 1955 and has now topped 200,000. The centre for current immigration and rural development plans is on the southern Huila plateau. The railway has been extended inland from Sá da Bandeira, hydro-electric and irrigation schemes are being undertaken on the Cunene river, and further *colonatos* being prepared. Out of a total of £36 million earmarked for Angola in the 1953 six-year Development Plan, over £27 million went to Huila.[5]

White settlement on the land has also been undertaken in Moçambique, although the climate is less suitable there and the numbers involved are not so high. Portugal clearly intends to extend the *colonato* system, particularly in the south of Angola. Since Portugal is committed to establishing the Portuguese way of life in Africa, since the colonists are forbidden to use African labour, and since in southern Angola there is a relative abundance of land, it is hoped that friction between Africans and Europeans will be kept to a minimum. Nevertheless, increased immigration is already creating discontent. The available funds are being spent on projects which benefit primarily the European colonists.[6] Job opportunities for Africans are decreasing as the number of poor white immigrants increase, some of whom drift to the cities rather than staying on the land. Many manual jobs are now taken by Portuguese immigrants and colour consciousness has already led to violent clashes in territories which at one time boasted a culture bar rather than a colour bar.

Angola is really five very different worlds – the old-established and hitherto easy-going coastal towns, the Diamang Concession in the far north-east, the sparsely settled and almost untouched eastern half of the country, the central and southern highlands with their unique experiment in mid twentieth century white settlement, and the plantation agriculture of the north.

In this last area, too, there is a tribal overlap with both Congo Republics. The area around the mouth of the Congo river is occupied by the Bakongo people whose memories go back to a united kingdom in the fifteenth and sixteenth centuries.

MOÇAMBIQUE

White colonization in Moçambique has been less effective, although there were in 1950 some 50,000 Europeans living in the colony, mostly in Lourenço Marques, a fine modern city which lives off the transit trade from the Rhodesias and the Republic of South Africa. Some agricultural *colonatos* have been started, but on a smaller scale than in Angola. The most notable is at Guijà on the Limpopo. Much of the country is low-lying and malarial, and there has been considerable emigration of workers into the Rhodesias, Malawi, and the Republic.

TABLE 23

Exports of Moçambique, 1961 (by value)

	per cent
Raw Cotton	27.0
Cashew nuts	13.3
Sugar	12.7
Copra	10.4
Tea	9.2
Sisal	9.0
Other	18.4
Total value 2,548 million escudos	

SOURCE: *U.N. Yearbook of International Trade Statistics 1961*, p. 439.

Moçambique is an essentially tropical country with a list of export crops notable more for their variety than their volume. It is clear that with a comprehensive investment programme and a settlement of political problems the country could one day play a much more significant role than has hitherto been the case.

SÃO TOMÉ AND PRINCIPE

Recent charges of forced labour in Angola[7] confirmed by a U.N. investigation have re-awakened interest in similar charges against Portugal early in this century;[8] charges which led among other things to a boycott by Cadbury Brothers of cocoa from São Tomé.

São Tomé and Principe are small islands lying some 200 miles off-shore from Gabon and Spanish Guinea.

Occupied by Portugal since the fifteenth century, they have a population of rather more than 60,000 and are organized for the production of cocoa and coffee on large plantations. Much of the labour (28,000 in 1950) is provided by Africans brought over from the mainland on four- or five-year contracts. They are paid a minimum wage equivalent to £1. 10s. a month, with free food, barrack lodging, and medical attention. Another source is the labour of prisoners and unconvicted detainees, of whom there are large numbers.

Although there is no colour bar, cultural and economic differences mean that there are in fact self-contained 'racial classes' with rigid occupational and social immobility. Efforts are being made to reform the contract labour system into a permanent one by means of grants of land.[9]

It is clear from the high value of exports per head of population* that São Tomé is one of the most likely places where charges of 'colonial exploitation' can be made to stick. The standard of living is no higher than in the rest of Portugal's colonies and the conclusion must be drawn that, whatever the liabilities of colonial ownership, São Tomé is for Portugal a very profitable piece of real estate.

THE EX-BELGIAN CONGO

Belgium's only colony† started out in 1908 with a legacy of misrule and maladministration from the Congo Free State of King Leopold. It moved through a period when it became the envy of some of its neighbours as a model of benevolent paternalism and, more recently, back again not so much to misrule as to chaos and international dispute.

Prior to the riots of January 1959 in Leopoldville, the Congo had indeed seemed miraculously peaceful and wonderfully prosperous. There were more and more children going to school, more and more hospitals – and no politics. Said the Belgian information service: 'It is true that no one votes in the Congo; they work. The Belgians prefer administration to politics.'[10] When politics did come, they came with devastating suddenness to a colony which was in many ways educated for 'work' but

*See Table 5, p. 77.
†Ruanda and Burundi, formerly Belgian-administered U.N. Trust Territories, are considered with East Africa in Chapter 11.

completely undeveloped for 'votes'. Belgium boasted of the fact that 40 per cent of school-age children were in school (compared with 19 per cent in the Rhodesias), but neglected to mention that less than 3,000 (1960) had completed more than seven years' schooling and that most of that schooling was in the local vernacular language.[11]

The absence of higher education and the use of the different tribal languages as the media for school instruction meant that such political consciousness as had developed was local and tribal rather than national, a factor furthered by the enormous size of the country – as big as Western Europe – and its relatively tiny population (14 million in 1961). Of this number, only about a million are urban. At the time of independence there were about 110,000 whites.

The Congo is dominated physically by the immense shallow depression known as the Congo Basin, and the extensive river system which drains it. Here, in the central and western areas, lie those thousands of square miles of sparsely inhabited equatorial forests which are often thought to characterize the whole. But the Congo is a land of great variety in the challenges and opportunities which are offered by a whole series of different environments.

Roughly south-east of a line drawn through Leopoldville, Luluabourg and Stanleyville, the dense forest ceases. Moving southwards, distances from the equator are great enough to bring about an increase in the length of the dry season, until ultimately the land rises to the high plateau of Katanga, where temperatures are considerably modified by altitude and the seasonal aridity of the land is intensified by poor and rocky soils.

To the east of the forest areas the land rises slowly and then spectacularly to the high, moist, but cool lands round the east African lakes of Kivu, Tanganyika, Edward, and Albert. Here are fertile plantations and tourist centres, which may one day rival more well-known places in popularity. Bukavu on Lake Kivu has been described as 'a combination of Lake Lucerne and the Bay of St Tropez'.[12]

The diverse parts of this great country are tied together by the Congo river system, both for transport and the actual or potential production of power.

The Congo river is fed by streams which arise some distance away on both sides of the equator. As a result some of the tributary streams are experiencing the Northern Hemisphere dry season at the same time as others are experiencing the Southern Hemisphere wet season – and *vice versa*. This means that the Congo-Lualaba main stream has one of the most even flows of any great river in the world.

As well as an even flow, the Congo is also noted for the falls and rapids which impede navigation at a number of points. Passing up-stream from the Atlantic, the first and major obstacle is a series of falls and rapids from the port of Matadi to Leopoldville at Stanley Pool. There is then a clear stretch of over 1,000 miles to Stanleyville, where navigation is again impeded – by Stanley Falls. From Ponthierville the river (now the Lualaba) is again navigable a further 200 miles to Kindu.

This combination of even flow and major navigation obstacles means that the Congo is an excellent source of hydro-electric power but that its usefulness as a major highway is severely limited. Nevertheless the Belgians succeeded in making the Congo and its tributaries into a major transport system by a series of linking railways to overcome the rapids and falls. Loading and unloading at the rail–river trans-shipment points is, of course, costly, but not as expensive as a more extensive railway network and the neglect of cheap water transport. The first linking railway to be built, finished in 1898, was the link from Matadi to Leopoldville, an essential prerequisite if the Congo Basin was to be opened to trade at all. The cost in money and lives (over 2,000) was great, but without it the Congo would have remained in isolation. Other links run from Stanleyville to Ponthierville, Port Franqui on the Kasai head of navigation to Katanga, Kindu to Kabalo, and, the most recent, from Kabalo to Katanga.

This coordination of river and rail transport links has been accompanied by the development of the Congo's different environments into a complementary economic whole. Rivers and railways link each productive area and provide lines of both urban and rural settlement between them.[13]

Some regions and provinces are heavily dependent on one or two export products, but taken as a whole the economy has been well diversified. If the Congo retains its unity, indeed, this diversified development will be a great asset for the future. If not, each region will be the poorer, or else far too dependent on one or two major commodities.

TABLE 24

Belgian Congo Exports (by value) in 1959 (excluding uranium)

	per cent
Copper	32.1
Coffee	12.9
Palm oil	6.5
Cobalt	6.3
Raw cotton	5.5
Tin	5.3
Diamonds	4.8

Total value 24 thousand million francs*

*This value dropped to 4 thousand million francs in 1960.

SOURCE: *U.N. Yearbook of International Trade Statistics 1960*, p. 144.

The life of Leopoldville province is centred on the ports of Leopoldville and Matadi, through which passes most of the Congo's trade. In addition there are some plantations for palm oil, cocoa, rubber, and coffee. Many of those for palm oil are controlled by Lever Brothers' subsidiary, the Compagnies des Huileries du Congo Belge.

The falls below Leopoldville have a tremendous hydro-electric potential as yet undeveloped; the Belgians preferred to build small barrages to serve the various industrial and urban centres. Although some coal is mined, most of the Congo's power is provided by these small barrages.

Kasai, north of Pt Franqui, and the south and east of Equator Province are the least developed and most impenetrable forest areas. South Kasai is the centre of the diamond industry, controlled by the Forminiere (Société Internationale Forestière et Minière du Congo) and satisfies nine tenths of the world demand for industrial diamonds.[14]

Eastern province, north of Stanleyville, is the largest area of European-owned plantations in the country, and is served by the 2 ft gauge Vicicongo railway (Société de Chemins de Fer Vicinaux du Congo). Cotton, coffee, palm oil, palm kernels, rice, and lumber all start their long journey from here, whence they are shipped down the Congo.

Eastern Province and Kivu have the best-balanced economies in the country and contain some of the most attractive and comfortable areas in which to live. Tin is mined in Kivu and at Manono in North Katanga, and there are plantations in Kivu for cinchona, tea, coffee, and pyrethrum. Even grapes are grown near Lake Kivu, giving two vintages a year from rich volcanic soils.

Katanga provides up to 60 per cent of the Congo's revenue at present,[15] with only some 17 per cent of the population, which fact alone helps to explain separatist tendencies. It is heavily dependent on its copper, cobalt, and uranium production, as not only are the soils poor but the Union Minière, unlike its counterparts in Zambia, has done little to encourage any agricultural activity.

Katanga is very much the creation of the Union Minière. It was a barren, thinly-peopled land before the company began to exploit the rich and easily-worked copper deposits. Many workers were imported from other parts of the Congo, and a deliberate policy of both settled labour and rapid African advancement in industrial skills was pursued. Alone among the provinces, Katanga need not rely on river transport. The railway routes to Lobito and Beira are cheaper than the all-Congo route. Even with government assistance and pressure to use the latter, less of Katanga's exports went through Leopoldville than from Beira and Lobito.[16]

The Congo was developed by Belgium as an economic whole. Much of it was well prepared for economic advance, but at the same time was kept politically mute. Inevitably this lack of political education and experience meant that local and tribal influences remained strong, while political movements dedicated to disrupting Congolese unity could combat those seeking to preserve it. Even the first and most important agitation for independence was not conducted by the unity-minded M.N.C. (Mouvement National Congolais) of Patrice Lumumba but by the tribal Abako party, representing the Bakongo tribe. In the elections of 1960 there were 110 competing political parties, most of them local and tribal groups. Only the M.N.C. – the largest single party – stood for national unity.

The other tribal party of some significance was the Conakat of M. Tshombe in Katanga. Supported by the Lunda and Bemba, as well as by most of the Europeans and industrialists in the province, it gained a narrow majority in the 1960 elections,[17] with the Balubas providing the main opposition (Balubakat) in the north. Both Lunda and Bemba extend into Zambia, but in the quite different political atmosphere in this British territory tribal nationalists are not very popular with local African politicians.

Belgium's mistakes have been so obvious and disastrous that it is easy to belittle the achievements. For much progress in the economic and social fields was made, particularly over the last decade. It is still fair comment on Belgian rule in the Congo to say that they were 'enlightened industrialists but short-sighted politicians'.[18]

Notes on Chapter 9

1. Quoted by J. Duffy in *Portuguese Africa*, 1959, p. 270.
2. Sá da Bandeira has 64.6 degrees F. mean annual temperature and 43 inches rain.
3. Duffy, op. cit., p. 49.
4. Salazar 1943, quoted in Duffy, op. cit., p. 337.
5. P. B. Stone, 'New Development in South Angola'. Article in *South African Geographical Journal*, December 1957.
6. ibid.
7. See Basil Davidson, *The African Awakening*, 1955.
8. H. W. Nevinson, *A Modern Slavery*, 1906.
9. R. J. Harrison Church, *West Africa*, p. 527.
10. Quoted by Colin Legum in 'What Went Wrong with the Congo', *Observer*, 14 August 1960.
11. Quoted by Clyde Sanger in the *Guardian*, 23 February 1961.
12. T. Marvel, *The New Congo*, 1949, p. 208.
13. The revolution in the life of Kasai brought about by the railway is discussed in H. Nicolai and J. Jacques, *La Transformation des Passages Congolais par le chemin de fer, l'exemple du BCK*, 1954.
14. Hailey. op. cit., p. 1516.
15. It is impossible to be more precise because of lack of information about uranium production.

---

16. 315,624 tons from Beira
    263,647 tons all Congo Route
    347,187 tons from Lobito

---

17. Congo Tribes and Parties. Royal Anthropological Institute, 1961. In the elections, Balubakat gained five seats in the Senate as against seven for Conakat. In the Chamber of Representatives Balubakat gained seven seats as against

eight for Conakat. See also Colin Legum, *Congo Disaster*,
Penguin Special, 1961.
18. Basil Davidson in *New Statesman and Nation*, 24 April 1954.
See also C. Hoskyns, *The Congo Since Independence*, 1964.

10 Rhodesia,* Malawi, and Zambia

These three countries were joined together in the Federation of Rhodesia and Nyasaland in 1953 amidst a storm of controversy both in Africa and in Britain. Advocates of Federation won the day largely on the economic arguments advanced: that the economies of the three territories were complementary and that they would be more prosperous together than apart. Opposition to Federation came from those with political objections, especially the Africans of Northern Rhodesia and Nyasaland. They feared that the effective control of Southern Rhodesia by the European minority and the system of segregation practised there would be extended northwards under a federal system. They argued that economic cooperation was possible without political union and that any economic advantages would be outweighed by political disadvantages.

Africans in Southern Rhodesia were somewhat less hostile to Federation, probably because they hoped their own position would be strengthened by association with the more liberal north. Some Europeans in Southern Rhodesia also opposed Federation on similar grounds, fearing that they would be swamped by the black majority in the northern territories.

After ten years the Federation has now been dismantled. Nyasaland has become the independent state of Malawi; Northern Rhodesia became the independent state of Zambia in October 1964, while the future of Rhodesia was still uncertain at the time of writing.

Political opposition to Federation had increased since 1953, especially among Africans in the north. The Monckton Commission[1] reported that they 'were left in no doubt that genuine opposition to Federation on the part of Africans in the Northern Territories has grown more intense.'[2] The Africans pointed out

*Former Southern Rhodesia was re-named Rhodesia in October 1964, on the independence of Zambia.

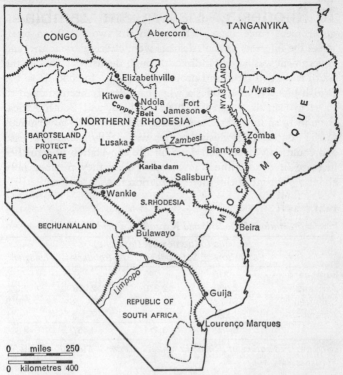

MAP 20. Former Central African Federation and Moçambique

that attachment to Federation had held up political progress and that this was more important than any possible economic advantages, which they tended to discount anyhow.

The breakdown of the conference of 1960, assembled to review the Federal Constitution, made it clear that further inter-territorial development was impossible until the future constitutions and direction of development of the individual territories had been worked out. The three territories certainly made strange political bedfellows.

Northern Rhodesia and Nyasaland were Protectorates, controlled ultimately by Governors appointed by the British Government. Southern Rhodesia's European minority rules itself. It is the largest of all the European communities in southern

Africa outside the Republic and has had full internal self-government since 1923. Whereas in the two Northern territories the interests of the Africans were clearly paramount, and government was largely indirect through the native chiefs, in the south it seemed right and proper – in 1923 – to concede to the British pioneers in Rhodesia what had already been granted to those in Canada, Australia, New Zealand, and South Africa. Even in 1923, however, the granting of internal self-government to the Southern Rhodesian whites was clearly a marginal case and could only have been done on the expectation of a further increase in the numbers involved. Today they number only about 7 per cent of the total population in that territory.

TABLE 25

Former Federation of Rhodesia and Nyasaland. Population Estimates 1960

| | *(in 000s to the nearest thousand)* | | | |
	Federation	*S. Rhodesia*	*N. Rhodesia*	*Nyasaland*
Europeans	312	225	77	10
Africans	8,080	2,870	2,370	2,840
Coloured	14	10	2	2
Asians	26	6	8	11
	8,432	3,111	2,457	2,836

SOURCE: *Federation of Rhodesia and Nyasaland Monthly Digest of Statistics July 1961.*

RHODESIA

Rhodesia is a land some two or three times as large as England and Wales but the productive wealth of the country is concentrated into less than half the total area. About one third is the unhealthy Low Veld, lying below 2,000 ft, much of it tsetse-infested and malarial and having an uncertain rainfall. The Low Veld covers large tracts of the country on both its northern and southern boundaries – along the Zambezi in the north and the Limpopo in the south.

The most important area is the High Veld (generally from four to five thousand feet), where a combination of altitude, good soils, adequate rainfall and some exploitable minerals have concentrated the population, both African and European. The

High Veld stretches from the south-west to the north-east, from the neighbourhood of Bulawayo to that of Salisbury. It is a fairly narrow strip, about 50 miles wide, covering about 20 per cent of the area of the country. North and east of Salisbury are two narrower extensions of the High Veld, both over 5,000 ft in altitude. The eastern extension is the larger and continues over the border into Moçambique.

The High Veld contains the line of rail* and the major towns. In the north-eastern area around Salisbury, rainfall is adequate (over 30 ins.) for crop cultivation, but in the south-west, in areas of 25 ins. of rainfall or less, ranching becomes more important. Here in the south-west are most of the country's important minerals, among them asbestos, chrome, and gold. Away from the High Veld the altitude of the plateau surface falls away on both sides to the Middle Veld (3,000–4,000 ft) and beyond that to the Low Veld.

The Middle Veld covers between 40 and 50 per cent of the total land area and although much of it is good land it has been less developed than the High Veld and it has poorer communications. Much of it is African-owned. Coal is found in the Middle Veld at Wankie in the north-west.

THE EUROPEAN POPULATION

The European population came to Southern Rhodesia as conquerors and the facts of that conquest have coloured their attitudes ever since.

Prior to the European occupation, much of the south and west of the country was under the rule of Lobengula, King of the Matabele. This warlike tribe was centred on the site of modern Bulawayo from where they forced their attentions and exercised their authority (by cattle raiding) over the less well organized Mashona to the north and east.

European penetration was initiated by Rhodes's British South Africa Company, which in 1888 succeeded in obtaining from Lobengula the right to mine minerals throughout his domains. The Company obtained a Royal Charter from the British

---

*Except that from Bulawayo through Wankie to Livingstone. This is the Middle Veld.

Government in the following year. Although the mineral concession contained no rights of settlement, Company rule was soon extended to the Mashona areas. By 1893 Lobengula himself was driven from his Kraal and the whole territory brought under Company rule.

This conquest is still seen today by white Rhodesians as part of a glorious Imperial past and is taught as such in Rhodesian schools. The national holidays of Rhodes Day, Founder's Day, Pioneer Day and others, all help to drive the point home. Moreover, the conquest is not seen as aggression but as a valiant pioneer struggle against natural obstacles – including the natives. In this respect it resembles the American view of their own 'manifest destiny' in occupying the whole of the United States, only in the case of Rhodesia there were an inconveniently large number of natives still left when the occupation was completed. Nevertheless, development assumed that Southern Rhodesia would remain solely a white man's country, an attitude which is only now beginning to change.

As E. Clegg puts it:

Economic development was thought of as being entirely in the hands of Europeans. They were creating a new world, their world. The African was needed as an instrument to help in that creation: he was not wanted as a permanent feature of it. His home was the tribal village. This attitude was not surprising. The African was a naked savage; his life bounded by the spear and primitive agriculture. To think of the differences between the races being bridged was to stretch human credulity unreasonably.[3]

Unfortunately for this point of view, the material differences between the races have narrowed, while the political gulf remains as wide as ever.

The structure of the European population has been analysed by Colin Leys.[4] Among other things, he points out that this population is still largely made up of immigrants as distinct from those who are Rhodesian born, and that urban manual workers form an important element in the community.

Over two thirds are immigrants, a majority of whom have moved into Rhodesia from Britain, having stayed some time in South Africa. In addition, schooling and university education as well as holidays are often taken there, so that the influence of South African racial ideas on the European community has been strong. In addition, most of the immigrants move into manual jobs where they have little social and economic security and where they are rapidly made aware of the potential economic competition of Africans.

TABLE NO. 27

European employment. Southern Rhodesia and England & Wales. 1951

Agricultural	Southern Rhodesia per cent	England & Wales per cent
1. Farmers	15·1	2·1
2. Farm workers	0.6	5·2
Non-Agricultural		
3. Professional and administrative workers, employers and shopkeepers	25·8	16·7
4. Clerical workers	10.8	5·1
5. Shop assistants	6·2	3·4
6. Skilled manual workers and foremen	38·5	40·5
7. Semi-skilled and unskilled manual workers	1·7	24·7

SOURCE: 1951 Population Censuses. Southern Rhodesia and U.K. Quoted in C. Leys. *European Politics in Southern Rhodesia*, 1959.

It will be seen from Table 26 that the three really striking differences between the Southern Rhodesian employment pattern and that of England and Wales are the larger number of farmers; the smaller number of farm workers, and the smaller number of unskilled and semi-skilled workers outside agriculture. These are, perhaps, what we should expect without access to statistics. A country which depends on agricultural exports may be expected to have a larger percentage of farmers than Britain, while the unskilled and semi-skilled work is mostly done by non-Europeans. What may be surprising to the outsider is that so many Europeans are engaged in manual work at all. This certainly has great political significance.

No less than 40.2 per cent of employed male Europeans are engaged in non-agricultural manual work. If some of the clerical workers and shop assistants are included, we can assume that nearly half the European population is dependent on jobs in which Africans are beginning to acquire skills and into which they demand entry. Many of these jobs have been 'traditionally' European, at rates of pay which a poor country like Rhodesia cannot afford on a mass scale. The standard of living of large numbers of Europeans would thus be directly threatened if entry to employment was made to depend entirely on ability. It is not yet an immediate threat to the whole of the skilled labour force, because the number of skilled Africans is still too few, but it could place a high proportion of European's jobs in jeopardy before many years have passed.

The racial division between unskilled and skilled work has been aided by the educational system. The education of whites is universal and free. The education of Africans, especially in secondary education, still lags far behind. State expenditure on education per head of population is twenty times as high for Europeans as for Africans,[5] although the amount for the latter is now being increased. Both in job reservation and in education the Europeans still form a privileged caste. Their privileges can only be maintained by the continuance of white political control.

The European population is essentially urban, the African still essentially rural, although the African drift to the towns is gathering momentum as industrialization proceeds. These urban areas are the centre of European life and the chief growing points of the economy, but land and land policy are still crucial.

The Land Apportionment Act of 1931 is the cornerstone of land policy and the basis of segregation in Southern Rhodesia. The Whitehead Government had been preparing to abolish it but it has been kept in force by his successors. Under its terms the whole country is divided into African and European areas, plus some areas of Crown land not yet allocated (mostly in the Low Veld). The European area (49 per cent of the whole) is a continuous belt of country along the lines of rail and contains all the main towns and most of the High Veld. The African areas are discontinuous tracts of land, mostly in the Middle Veld.

The allocation of land under the Act was based on false assumptions about future African needs for land which left no room for future expansion. It was assumed that European enterprise would grow: African farming would remain static. Moreover, those Africans living in the European area were

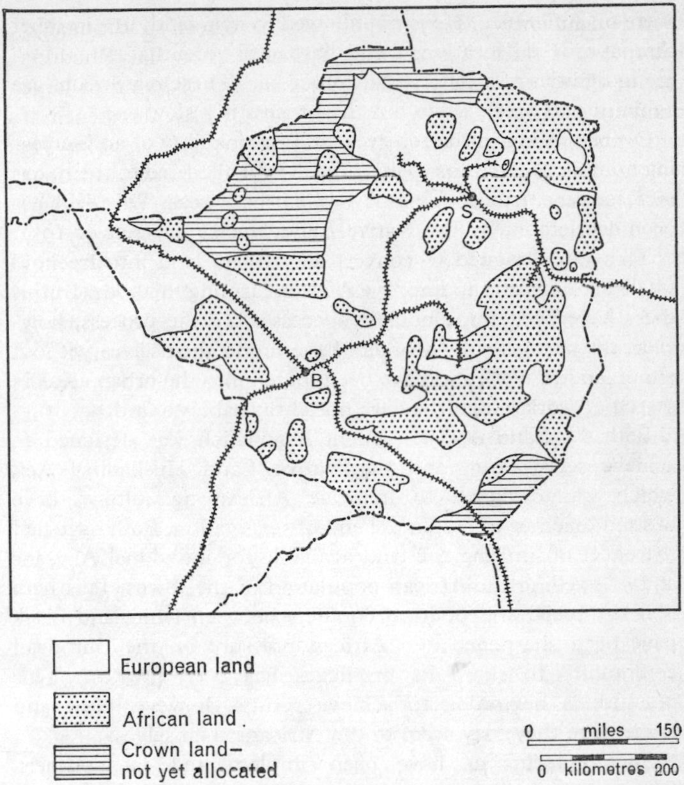

European land

African land .

Crown land—
not yet allocated

0   miles   150

0   kilometres   200

MAP 21. Southern Rhodesia: division of land under the 1931 Land Apportionment Act

gradually to be removed to the areas reserved for native purchase.[7] Already by 1939, however, the number of African farmers in the areas reserved to them exceeded the 1931 estimates and the African areas were becoming seriously overcrowded. This has not prevented the continuing resettlement of Africans from empty lands into the overcrowded reserves, a process which was still going on as late as 1958.[8]

The Land Apportionment Act has also slowed down the integration of non-Europeans into urban life. Under its terms the towns are in the white areas and the African comes to work there on sufferance. He is not allowed to own land, live in other than approved 'locations', and has, until recently, suffered all the indignities of a rigid social colour bar. These restrictions are beginning to break down but the process is a slow one.[9]

Overcrowding in the reserves, and the inability of an increasing number of Africans to live off the land allocated to them, has increased the drift of Africans to the urban areas. This drift has been accelerated by the Native Land Husbandry Act of 1951.

This was designed to convert all African land into freehold small-holdings and to improve African farming methods. In this there have been some notable successes. In the process, however, the surplus rural workers have found themselves without either land or work and have been forced into the urban areas in search of work which they are not always able to find.

Both the Land Apportionment Act, which was designed to achieve segregation, and the Native Land Husbandry Act, which was designed to improve African agriculture, have worked together to hasten the end of segregation. Both have had the effect of limiting the land available for individual Africans and of swelling the African population of the towns. It is here that the social and political conflicts between white and black have been sharpened and African pressure on the European community to share its privileges has been greatest. This pressure is beginning to achieve results, however slow and inadequate they may seem to the Africans themselves.

Such reforms as have been implemented in Southern Rhodesia have been too few and too late to convince the Africans of the two northern territories that they wish to be associated with a Rhodesia ruled by Europeans.

MALAWI

This is overwhelmingly the poorest of the three countries and is dependent for its livelihood both on the production of its own agriculture and the annual export of labour to work in the mines industries, and farms of Zambia, Rhodesia, and the Republic. Up to one third of the adult male labour force is away from home at any one time.[10]

In 1959 the Gross Domestic Product of Nyasaland was £19 a head, of Northern Rhodesia £81 and of Southern Rhodesia £89. Without any exploitable mineral resources, with long and expensive communications, a peasant population swollen by continuing immigration from Portuguese Territories and with restricted scope for European enterprise ... and for the employment which such enterprise offers, the economic opportunities open to Africans are few.[11]

Malawi is like Uganda in having been penetrated by missionaries before a Protectorate was established. Scottish missions were active from the 1870s and, before the coming of official British rule in 1891, sometimes acted as the government. Slave raiding and inter-tribal strife had so broken down the old tribal structure that the missions found themselves in the position not of replacing an existing government but of providing government where none existed.

Malawi is a land of very varied relief and consequently of climate. Three main types of terrain may be distinguished. The hot and unhealthy lowlands of the Shire river and the shores of Lake Nyasa, the cooler plateaux, between three and four thousand feet, and the still higher plateaux between five and eight thousand feet. Maize is the staple diet on the plateaux and cassava on the Lake shore.

Population, both African and European, is concentrated in the southern highlands. Communications are good here, soils are fertile and the climate pleasant for human comfort. Land alienated to white farmers (about 5 per cent of the whole country) is mainly concentrated in the south.

The chief cash crops of tobacco, tea, groundnuts, coffee, and cotton are produced both on the European-owned farms and by African farmers. The latter are mostly smallholders in a transition stage between subsistence and commercial agriculture. Supplementation of a predominantly subsistence holding by some cash crop is common.

TABLE 27

Malawi. Exports in 1959 (by value)

	per cent
Tobacco	50
Tea	41
Other	9

SOURCE: *Colonial Office Annual Report 1959.*

ZAMBIA

The former Protectorate of Northern Rhodesia lies between Nyasaland and Southern Rhodesia, both geographically and economically. Much of the country is too remote from good communications to have seen much development, and is still largely devoted to subsistence agriculture. There is, however, a zone of more intensive development – both in agriculture and in mining – along the line of rail.

Most of Zambia is high plateau country on the watershed between the Congo and the Zambesi, having a tropical climate modified by altitude. It is hotter than the High Veld of Southern Rhodesia, but only the valleys of the Zambesi and Luangwa are excessively hot. It has not, however, the climatic attractions for Europeans offered by the more favoured areas of its southern neighbour.

Except along the line of rail, European settlement and commercial farming are confined to two small areas; one near Abercorn in the North, which looks to Tanganyika for its contacts with external markets, and the other near Fort Jameson, whose communications are mainly through Malawi.

The Copperbelt lies between Broken Hill and the Congo border, and is a continuation of a similar area in Katanga. Its development has created the wealth and many of the political problems of Northern Rhodesia. The first mine, at Bwana Mkubwa, produced low-grade copper in the 1920s, but it was with the discovery of far richer deposits and the beginnings of their exploitation in 1931 that the story of the Copperbelt really begins.

In the 1920s European miners were brought in by the mining companies at relatively high wages because at that time no suitable local labour existed, except for the unskilled work. These miners, through the Northern Rhodesia Mineworkers' Union (an entirely European body, formed in 1926) have been able to consolidate their position and, until recently, to monopolize all the skilled work at rates of pay about ten times as high as those for unskilled work. They thus had the same direct economic interest in the continuance of white political control as have the manual workers of Southern Rhodesia,[12] and continued to resist, with decreasing effectiveness, the growing strength of African nationalism.

There are seven main mines on the Copperbelt, producing copper and much smaller quantities of zinc, cobalt, gold, silver, lead, and manganese. So one-sided has been the economic development of the country that well over half the Africans in employment are working in or near the Copperbelt.[13] Most of the commercial agriculture is concentrated along the railway which serves the Copperbelt and is largely a supplier of the domestic market, although small quantities of groundnuts and tobacco are produced for export.

TABLE 28

Zambia. Mineral output in 1961 (by value)

	millions
Copper	£114·6
Zinc	2·2
Cobalt	1·9
Lead	1·0
Manganese	0.4
Other	1·0

SOURCE: *Statesman's Yearbook 1963.*

The Copperbelt has attracted not only immigrant Europeans, but also somewhat larger numbers of Africans from outside Zambia, many of them from Malawi, and the Portuguese Territories.

TABLE 29

Adult male Employees in mining and quarrying 1956

Africans from:	
Northern Rhodesia	27,417
Nyasaland	4,175
Southern Rhodesia	73
Portuguese Territories	1,168
Others	4,502
Europeans	6,159

SOURCE: Federation of Rhodesia & Nyasaland, 1956 Census.

THE ECONOMY OF THE FORMER FEDERATION

The complementary nature of the economies of the three former Federal Territories has often been stressed. A common market of eight and a half million people ought also to have grown faster than three smaller ones and have greater credit-worthiness. As the Monckton Report put it:

The more advanced agriculture and light industries of Southern Rhodesia are balanced by the heavy extractive industry in Northern Rhodesia and vice versa; coal from Wankie is used to smelt copper in Northern Rhodesia and the railway system transports both; tea from Nyasaland is drunk in Salisbury; meat raised in Matabeleland is eaten on the Copperbelt . . .

It is true, too, that measured by investment rates and growth in exports, the economy has expanded since Federation to a remarkable degree.[15] Growth has, however, been very uneven and has served to increase contrasts in wealth between people and regions. Moreover it has not helped to reduce dependence on a very small number of export commodities.

Most of the investment in the Federation went into the building of Kariba dam and into the industries of Southern Rhodesia; industries which, because of the Federation's poor and lengthy communications, are inevitably concerned with supplying the domestic market.

Under careful government protection, Southern Rhodesia has been able to build up a remarkable range of industries. Among them are the first iron and steel works in southern Africa outside the Republic, textiles, cement, agricultural implements, food and drink, soap, paints, and tyres. These are concentrated in and around Salisbury and Bulawayo and have been able to grow because of the high cost of imports and the necessity to absorb European immigrants.

Of the former Federation's exports, over two thirds by value were of two commodities – Northern Rhodesian copper (47.3 per cent) and Southern Rhodesian tobacco (19.5 per cent).[15] But both the production of export commodities and the new industrial growth bear little relation to the production and income of the vast majority of the inhabitants – those still engaged in subsistence or semi-subsistence agriculture. Most of them were quite unimpressed, therefore, when told of the Federation's economic achievements. As two African members of the Monckton Commission have put it:

It is true to say that the economic advantages which have accrued from the Federation resulted in high standards of living for Europeans . . . and created some employment for Africans in Southern Rhodesia and Nyasaland . . .

It is wrong in our view for the Commission, when dealing with Kariba, to say that Africans were going to benefit as a result of this hydro-electric scheme. The Commission visited most of the African municipal townships . . . and saw that in the majority of cases hardly any of these townships were supplied with electricity at all . . .[16]

The former Federal Territories have yet to work out their economic future and degree of cooperation. Malawi is still poor and will still need to export her labour for some time to come. Zambia is poor, too, but has the enormous advantage of plenty of income for investment from the mines. If the proposed railway through Tanganyika becomes a reality,* then that country may also expect to receive a boost to her investment income.

The biggest immediate economic problem faces Southern Rhodesia, a country whose economy has depended on a Federal market which has now disappeared. In order to maintain her prosperity, Southern Rhodesia must forge new links with either the Republic of South Africa or with Zambia and Malawi. But the economic problem is also a political problem. What solution is found will depend on political developments in the immediate future.

*Projected for political reasons to avoid the Portuguese Territories as outlets to the sea.

Notes on Chapter 10

1. *Report of the Advisory Commission on the Review of the Constitution of Rhodesia and Nyasaland.* 1960 Cmnd. 1148.
2. ibid., pp. 17–18.
3. E. Clegg, *Race and Politics*, 1960, p. 33.
4. In *European Politics in Southern Rhodesia.* 1959.
5. Philip Mason, *Year of Decision*, 1960, pp. 187–8.
6. ibid., pp. 170–71.
7. African land was divided into the 'reserves' and 'native purchase areas'. In the latter, freehold tenure was introduced and attempts were made to improve farming methods.
8. This, and other effects of the Land Apportionment Act are fully considered in R. Gray, *The Two Nations*, 1960, and Philip Mason, op. cit.
9. As, for example, the abolition of separate counters in P.O.s and the building of permanent urban housing for Africans on ninety-nine year leases.
10. *Report of the Nyasaland Commission of Enquiry (Devlin Report)*, 1959, pp. 7–8.
11. *Monckton Commission Report*, p. 57.
12. For a short history of the industrial colour bar see *World Today*, May 1955, and E. Clegg, op. cit.
13. *Colonial Office. N. Rhodesia Annual Report*, 1960, p. 13.
14. ibid., p. 23.
15. *U.N. Economical Survey of Africa since 1950*, p. 168.
16. *Monckton Commission Report*, p. 135.

East Africa
11 Kenya, Uganda, Tanganyika, Zanzibar, Ruanda and Burundi

East Africa is a land of great variety; in physical features, climate, human types, economic development, and political evolution alike. There are few places on the earth's surface where, in the space of a few hundred miles, you can experience such a range of contrasts. You can pass from high mountain snows to the deepest lake-filled troughs lined with tropical vegetation; from the invigorating climate of the highland areas to the dusty heat of the rift valley floors, or from bustling modern cities to a countryside still largely devoted to subsistence agriculture. It would, moreover, be false to make a firm distinction between developed towns and an underdeveloped countryside. There are great differences between one area and another. Particularly in Kenya, you can move from a fully commercial agriculture to the poorest subsistence farming or from fertile volcanic soils, like those round Kilimanjaro in Tanganyika, to the poor and eroded pastures of the Masai on the floor and margins of the rift valley. Finally, there are in East Africa all the clashes of tribal and racial interests present in other parts of the continent and great contrasts in the types of state which have emerged from the race to independence.

These diverse environments and their many difficult problems have been given a certain unity by two facts, one physical and the other political.

Away from the coast, the encircling arms of the eastern and western rift valley systems are a unique feature of the African physical scene and are responsible for many of the region's physical and human contrasts. The western rift mountains and lakes cut east Africa off from the Congo Basin and from Northern Rhodesia, while the eastern and western rift highlands alike contain fertile volcanic soils and some of Africa's highest population densities. In between the two arms the plateau surface centres on the fertile, well watered and thickly populated Lake Victoria depression.

Politically, with the exception of Ruanda and Burundi, all the territories have been under British rule and use English as an official language.* Most of Kenya was a Crown Colony, except the coastal strip which was a Protectorate; Uganda and Zanzibar were Protectorates, while Tanganyika has been administered by Britain under U.N. Trusteeship. Both Tanganyika and Ruanda Burundi were German colonies in the years before the First World War but Belgium became the administering power for the latter country and tended, until recently, to make little distinction between Ruanda/Burundi and the colony of Congo. The British territories have enjoyed common tariff arrangements and certain common services, like railways, administered by the E.A.C.S.O.† How much of these common services and arrangements will be preserved after the withdrawal of British power is one of the important questions to be settled in the immediate future.

LAND AND CLIMATE

East Africa may conveniently be divided into five natural regions which, as so often throughout the continent, cut right across the political boundaries.

The coastal fringe, varying in width from ten to forty miles, has an equatorial climate with abundant though not excessive rain and accompanying tropical vegetation. This part of east Africa has had centuries of contact with the outside world, contact which is reflected in the cosmopolitan racial, cultural, and architectural character of the cities of the coast.

Prior to the coming of British and German rule the coast was controlled by the Sultan of Zanzibar. Germany bought the Tanganyika coast for £200,000 in 1890, but the Kenya coast became a protectorate over which the Sultan of Zanzibar still had some claim until 1963.

The coastal hinterland, for the most part dry and uninviting,

---

*Kenya and Tanzania also use Swahili.

†East African Common Services Organization, formerly the East African High Commission. See below.

cuts off the coast from the great population centres of the interior. Whereas the coast has long been known to the outside world the inland areas were only well known towards the end of the nineteenth century. In Kenya the zone is one of semi-desert and in most of the long rail haul from Mombasa to Nairobi (about 300 miles) there are few people and little economic activity. This dry zone becomes more marked as you move northwards in Kenya and the whole northern half of the country is semi-desert or desert. In Tanganyika the coastal hinterland is better watered and inland from Tanga contains the extensive sisal estates which are the country's principal source of developed wealth.

The highlands of the eastern rift, mainly over 5,000 ft, are a discontinuous zone with many natural advantages of soil and climate. Temperatures are comfortably modified by the altitude, the soils are deep and, like most volcanic soils, have a valuable reserve of natural fertility when not abused. The climate and the crops grown tend to vary with altitude rather than with season or latitude and there may be great variety within a small area. In the Kenya Highlands, for example, you can see wheat, oats, barley, pyrethrum,* tea, coffee, and pineapples all flourishing within a few miles of each other.

The western rift highlands of Ruanda, Burundi and Western Uganda are less well known and, because of their distance from the sea, less developed. They are, however, naturally fertile and support a dense African population. Ruanda and Burundi have nearly five million people (1960), more than the whole of Angola.

The interior plateau, lying between the two rift systems and about 4,000 ft above sea level, is largely arid or semi-arid bush country, much of it infested with tsetse fly. The chief exception to the general aridity is the land on the margins of Lake Victoria. The lake has considerable local influence in producing a climate with a well-distributed rainfall. As a result, the Nyanza province of Kenya, the southern half of Uganda and, to a smaller extent, the lake shores of Tanganyika are able to support a dense and relatively prosperous African population.

It will already be evident from this description that there are considerable areas of east Africa too dry for successful farming. The East Africa Royal Commission estimated that a fair

*A daisy-like flower used in the making of insecticides.

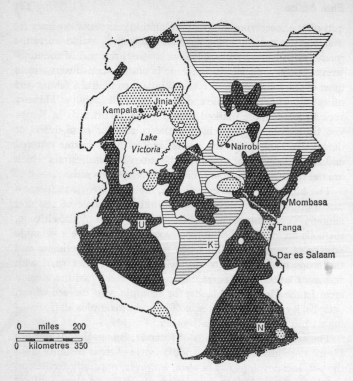

Areas which have a poor chance of having 30 ins. of rain a year *and* are infested with tsetse fly

Non-tsetse areas with a poor chance of 20 ins. of rain a year

Districts with over 100 persons per square mile

Ground-nut Scheme Centres

K=Kongwa

N=Nachingwea

U=Urambo

●—·—· Political boundaries

MAP 22. Kenya, Uganda, and Tanganyika: population, rainfall, and tsetse fly. (Sources: *E. Africa Royal Commission Report*, 1955; 'Exporting to East Africa', *Board of Trade Journal*, 25 August 1961, p. 5)

prospect of receiving 20 inches of rain a year was necessary for successful ranching and a fair prospect of 30 inches of rain a year was necessary for successful arable farming. Considerable areas do not measure up to these standards. In addition, much land which might otherwise be suitable for cattle is infested with tsetse fly. Some 10 per cent of Kenya, 32 per cent of Uganda, and 60 per cent of Tanganyika is tsetse-infested.[1]

The areas of extreme difficulty are illustrated in Map 22. Areas which have both a poor chance of 30 inches of rain and tsetse infestation are useless for both arable farming and cattle ranching. Areas with less than 20 inches are also useless without irrigation.[2] Small wonder that the people of east Africa are scattered in islands of high density in those areas which are more favourable to human activity.

Contrasts between the fertile and the infertile, the well-watered and the arid, are so great in east Africa that land hunger and competition for land are pressing problems, especially in Kenya. The position was summed up by the East Africa Royal Commission in 1955 as follows:

If a panorama picture could be taken slowly, and over a period, of the way people are living in East Africa, the most striking feature of it would be a restless anxiety to obtain and hold on to the land. Land is still, for the vast majority, a basic necessity from which each family derives its own food by its own physical effort. Where this can be done with the least effort for the greatest result, people have tended to collect and tend to want to stay. This tendency has been accentuated by the difficulty of penetrating the unknown where tsetse and lack of water have proved insurmountable obstacles, and by the hazards of uncertain rainfall over such a large part of the region. Thus the places where good rainfall, good soil, water and grazing are most easily obtained, the risks of human and animal disease most easily avoided, are in the greatest demand. As population has increased – and this has generally been greatest in these most favourable localities – so has pressure increased in two directions, outwards, so as to get more land if possible and to obtain as fertile land as possible, and inwards, towards a more devastating use of the land itself. The inward pressure, under contemporary systems of land usage, is affecting production from the soil adversely. This is the most serious aspect of the land problem. The outward pressure results in conflict wherever fertile land is short . . .[3]

PEOPLES AND POLITICS IN KENYA, UGANDA
AND TANGANYIKA

TABLE 30

Population of Kenya, Uganda, Tanganyika, and Zanzibar, mid 1962 estimates (in 000's)

	Africans	Europeans	Arabs and Asians	Total
Kenya	8,393	66	213	8,676
Uganda	6,920	11.2	82.1	7,016
Tanganyika	9,419	21.4	115.1	9,560
Zanzibar (1958)	295*	0.62	19.86†	315
Total	25,027	99.22	430.06	25,557

*Indigenous inhabitants (Arabs, Africans, and Cormorians).
†Excluding Arabs but including Somalis.

SOURCE: *East African Economic and Statistical Review*, March 1963.

Contrasts in the land and the distribution of population are paralleled by contrasts in the people themselves. Not only are there several immigrant groups to contend with – notably the Europeans, Asians, and Arabs – but the differences between the African tribes in language and political outlook are just as important in some areas.

East Africa is the meeting point for all the continent's major linguistic groups. Even the 'click' languages are represented in central Tanganyika. The three groups of greatest importance are the Nilotic, the Nilo-Hamitic, and the Bantu, and of these the latter are by far the most important. Of the tribes whose numbers are around the million mark only the Luo are a non-Bantu people.

The political importance of tribal differences varies greatly in the three territories. Tribalism appears to be unimportant in Tanganyika, important in the case of one major tribe in Uganda, and, immediately prior to independence, seemed a seriously divisive factor in Kenya.

In Tanganyika there are between 80 and 120 tribal groups, none of whom is numerically anywhere near the million mark except the Sukuma of the southern shores of Lake Victoria.

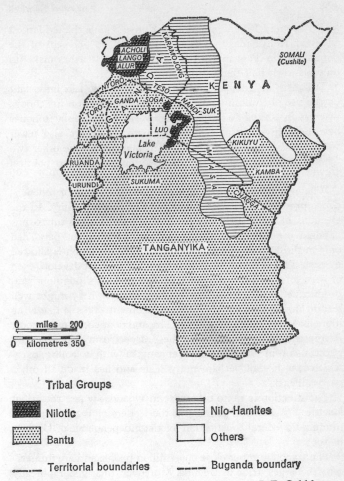

MAP 23. East Africa: Major tribal groups. (Source: J. E. Goldthorpe and F. B. Wilson, *Tribal Maps of East Africa and Zanzibar*, 1960)

Unlike some of the important tribes of Kenya and Uganda, the geographical situation of the Sukuma makes them remote from the capital city and centre of political activity. Partly for this reason, there has never been any question or fear of Sukuma political domination as there is of Baganda domination in Uganda or Kikuyu and Luo domination in Kenya. While the ten largest tribes of Kenya make up between 80 and 90 per cent of the population, in Tanganyika the fourteen biggest tribes make up only just over half the population.[4]

Tribalism in Tanganyika has also been made less important by the use of Swahili as the language of instruction in schools, whereas in Kenya and Uganda the various vernacular tongues have been given greater encouragement; there are also fewer trained and educated leaders in Tanganyika than the other two territories and therefore less competition for the top political jobs.

Whatever the reasons, Tanganyika on the verge of independence presented a remarkable picture of political unity. In the elections of 1960 no fewer than fifty-eight seats went to unopposed candidates of T.A.N.U.,* an achievement paralleled only in those countries where no effective opposition is allowed to exist. This is not to say that opposition will not develop, even of a regional kind. The fact that Tanganyika's populous and productive areas are scattered around its periphery might well lead to the emergence of regional discontent. This is made the more likely by the country's great size and poor communications. At present, however, we have the prospect of a strong central government in independent Tanganyika with a ruling party which now has all parliamentary seats and has made all other parties illegal.

The situation is quite otherwise in Uganda, where the tribal loyalties and political acumen of the leaders of Buganda† have produced a federal constitution for the independence of Uganda in 1962.

The Ganda number close on a million people and are numerically the largest tribe in Uganda. Moreover, their geographically central position places them at the centre of economic and political power. The capital city and seat of government are in Buganda, the country's road system radiates out from Buganda

*Tanganyika African National Union.

†Buganda, or the country of the Ganda, has given a modified form of its name to the whole of Uganda almost by accident. Buganda was the first part of Uganda to fall under British rule and was called 'Uganda' by the early administrators. As other bits and pieces of country were added, the name Uganda came to apply to the whole protectorate and the country of the Ganda was given its proper name, Buganda.

and the comparative wealth of the Ganda people has brought them greater educational and job opportunities than other tribes. The average money income per head of Africans in central Buganda is nearly ten times as great as in parts of the Western Province and over twice as much as that in most other parts of the country.[5]

Buganda's position of wealth and influence, which is due in part to this favourable geographical situation, has also been strengthened by British colonial policy.

When a British Protectorate was established in 1900 it was convenient for Britain to control the country through the existing native administration. The agreement between Britain and the Kabaka's government not only confirmed the authority of that government but gave it a status far above that of the surrounding tribes. More than this, the Ganda were rewarded for their loyalty by British recognition of the annexation of territory from the less co-operative Nyoro. This annexation has given rise to the present 'lost counties' dispute.

The claims of Bunyoro extend to five of the northern counties of Buganda and parts of two others, all of them claimed on historical grounds as once forming part of the lands of the Nyoro people. The dispute really centres on the three north-western counties in two of which (Buyaga and Bugangazzi) the Nyoro form an overwhelming majority of the population. For some decades prior to British rule Buganda had been expanding at the expense of Bunyoro so that two or three of the counties would probably have passed to Buganda without British intervention. It is doubtful, however, whether Buganda would have been able to acquire Buyaga and Bugangazzi when it did without British help.*

The strength of the feelings aroused by this dispute, not only between the main contestants but among the other tribes of Uganda, is a measure of the suspicions of some other tribes of Buganda's intentions.

There is . . . a distinct danger that the dispute over the 'lost counties' might become a *casus belli* involving other parts of Uganda. Bunyoro has strong traditional connexions with the tribes of the

*The Molson Commission recommended the return of these two counties to Bunyoro in May 1962. The 1964 referendum has confirmed this.

Northern Province, which in general are hostile to Buganda's pretensions. It is possible that the north would support Bunyoro against Buganda and that civil war would result.[6]

Buganda is also suspicious in her turn of the infiltration of other tribes into Buganda. The 1959 census showed no less than 47 per cent of the population of the province to be natives of other areas. African immigrants have poured into Buganda in the last forty years in response to the greater economic opportunities existing there. They come from Ruanda, Burundi, and Tanganyika as well as other parts of Uganda and work as unskilled labourers on various construction works, non-African industrial enterprises and, for the Ganda themselves, on the land. Many return home but, as with immigrant groups the world over, an increasing proportion will stay. The birth rate of many of the immigrant tribes is higher than that of the Ganda and it will not be long, at present rates of increase and immigration, before the Ganda are a minority in their own country.

The new federal constitution safeguards the position of Ganda traditional institutions which might have been threatened by immigration and by modern political parties voted into power by the other provinces. And it places Buganda in an even stronger political position than before. It may, however, effectively disfranchise the members of immigrant tribes in Buganda. Certainly a great deal of tribal suspicion will continue to exist. The new constitution is, nevertheless, an expression on all sides of an intention to co-operate. Without such co-operation the future would be bleak indeed.*

In Kenya, the larger and economically more advanced tribes – notably the Kikuyu and the Luo – tended to support the party which demanded strong central government (K.A.N.U.). Many of the smaller tribes tended to support the party of 'democratic regionalism' (K.A.D.U.). Kenya's main concentrations of population are in three widely separated centres, the Mombasa district, the highlands near Nairobi (the home of the Kikuyu) and Nyanza Province (the home of the Luo and others). Each area has different languages, tribes, and economic problems. It would in any case be difficult to weld them into a cohesive

*The election of the Kabaka of Buganda as President of Uganda (1963) has reduced tension between Buganda and the rest of the country.

political whole. Without a strong government at the centre the task appears impossible.* Whatever happens in the future, however, there is no doubt that in the past the politics of Kenya have been dominated by its most influential but by no means most numerous 'tribe', the Europeans.

The Europeans in Kenya number some 66,000 people or about one in 100 of the total population. Although they nearly doubled their numbers between 1950 and 1960, they no longer control Kenya's political life and there future is uncertain. As elsewhere in east Africa, most of them live in the towns, especially Nairobi, and it is a myth to think of them as mainly settlers on the land.

The myth had some substance in the early days of white settlement. Europeans were brought in to farm on the Kenya highlands as a direct result of the building of the Uganda railway, which reached the site of modern Nairobi in 1899 and Kisumu in 1901. The railway had been built to reach the strategic headwaters of the Nile, to open up Uganda to legitimate trade, and to provide support for the Christian missions there. It was, however, a costly undertaking in both lives and money and, partly in order to make it pay, attention was soon directed to developing the highland areas of Kenya through which the railway passed. Under the stimulus provided by the enthusiasm of Lord Delamere and others, European farmers were encouraged to take up land on favourable terms from 1902 onwards and again, under special schemes for ex-servicemen, after the two world wars.

It has always been a small community – growing from just over 5,000 in 1914 to nearly 17,000 in 1931. In 1931 the largest occupational group was still in agriculture but was already being overtaken by government service and commerce. In 1948, out of the total 'gainfully employed' population, only 23 per cent were in agriculture and fishing. Government service, commerce, the

*Such a government has emerged since independence and has succeeded in reducing regional opposition to the minimum necessary for effective cohesion. It has recently achieved a one-party system by agreement.

The independence constitution of 1963 divided the country into seven Regions and the Nairobi area. One region (the North East) is claimed by Somalia as part of 'Greater Somalia'. The majority of the people of this region are Somalis (as is the case with the Ogaden of Ethiopia). 'Shifta' bandits from Somalia have been an increasing terrorist menace to North East Kenya in recent years.

professions and clerical occupations together accounted for over 62 per cent of the European population.

Nevertheless, in spite of the small numbers of people involved in farming, the land question has continued to be of immense importance in Kenya politics. Alienation of the former 'white highlands' formed the basis of race segregation in Kenya, just as the Land Apportionment Act still does in Southern Rhodesia. It made Nairobi primarily a non-African town and squeezed the Kikuyu between two sectors of European land, into their increasingly overcrowded reserve. It helped to sustain the Mau Mau rebellion and has resulted in exceedingly uneven economic development. Much money and skill has been put into the land in the European areas while only recently has much money and effort been devoted to improving the African areas.

In Tanganyika about 15 per cent of Europeans are in agriculture[7] but their diverse ethnic origins (Greeks, Germans, and English among others), their peripheral location and their remoteness from the political and commercial capital of the country have combined to reduce their political influence. In Uganda only a handful of Europeans are planters, most of the rest of them being employed in Government and other service occupations.

The Asian community has been established in east Africa for longer than many of the African tribes themselves. The myth of the Kenya Europeans as largely 'settlers' is paralleled by the myth of Asians as largely descended from labourers brought in to build the Uganda railway.[8] Arab traders have been on the coast for close on two thousand years and Indians have probably been there for nearly as long. It would indeed be surprising if they had not.

The geographical unity of the Indian Ocean, and the ancient navigation routes across it based on regularly changing monsoon winds, means that the east African coast has always provided bases for the brisk trading activities of the area. As elsewhere in Africa, the settlements remained coastal until the nineteenth century, but the enterprise and civilization established there, though cosmopolitan, was essentially Asian and has left its mark on all the cities of east Africa which have developed since the opening up of the interior. 'Asian' in East Africa usually means either Indian or Pakistani, Moslem or Hindu, as well as the smaller Goan Catholic group.* Arabs are, for many purposes, also included.

The Asians have come and continue to come to East Africa because of opportunities for trade and the advantages of a better life for themselves and their children. Their contribution to the economic development of the area has been out of all proportion to their numbers.

Whereas the European has gone in to east Africa to govern, to farm, or to engage in some relatively large-scale business enterprise, the small Asian shopkeeper has penetrated right out into the villages, creating a demand for goods where none existed before, providing most of the people's needs in consumer goods and, later, sometimes branching out into larger manufacturing or farming enterprises, as in cotton ginning or the sugar plantations of Uganda.

Whereas most Europeans were more or less temporary residents, the Asians had come to stay. They may have thought of India or Pakistan as 'home', but this was more a sentimental than a real attachment. With the coming of independence, however, Asian immigration has decreased and emigration increased.

Two factors combine to make the Asians an object of prejudice from Africans and from Europeans. One is social and the other economic.

Many Asians are closely involved with one or other of the Asian religious sects, most of which are exclusive to themselves.[9] They thus tend to have their own independent social and cultural life and to be cut off from many of the people among whom they live.

They are also concentrated in occupations which arouse popular envy. Characteristically they are shopkeepers and businessmen. In Tanganyika about 50 per cent of Asians are dependent on trade, in Kenya over 33 per cent, and in Uganda over 50 per cent.[10] In both these respects they are like the Jews of Europe and are in the same danger of being subjected to discrimination.† This danger needs to be closely watched both by

*From Goa, a former Portuguese enclave in India.

†For some evidence of prejudice see Paul Fordham and H. C. Wiltshire, 'Some Tests of Prejudice in an East African Adult College', Race, October 1963.

the Asians themselves and by the new African governments.
The Asian comes to east Africa to better himself and he usually
succeeds. In doing so he also helps to improve east Africa. As the
East Africa Royal Commission said:

... the remarkable tenacity and courage of the Indian trader has
been mainly responsible for stimulating the wants of the indigenous
peoples, even in the remotest areas, by opening to them a shop-
window on the modern world and for collecting for sale elsewhere
whatever small surpluses are available for disposal. The non-African
trading system as it exists in East Africa is one of the most important
assets which the economy possesses ...[11]

ECONOMIC DEVELOPMENT IN KENYA, UGANDA, AND TANGANYIKA

All three territories are still primarily agricultural countries.
They rely for their main source of wealth on the export of a few
important crops, although both Uganda and Tanganyika have
the beginnings of both mining and manufacturing industry and
Kenya has a fast-growing variety of manufactures, mainly of
consumer goods for the local east African market.

In Kenya much of the export production in agriculture comes
from European farms in the former 'white highlands' although
Africans are now to an increasing extent participating in the
money economy. This participation is a direct result of the land
reforms of the last ten years and of the adoption of the improved
techniques with which they have been associated.

African farmers have begun in Kenya a process which has
hardly started in Tanganyika and Uganda – the raising of output
per man and per acre on the available agricultural land. If purchasing power is to be increased sufficiently to sustain a developing manufacturing industry it will be essential to raise farm
incomes in all three territories. In spite of worsening terms of
trade in the main export commodities, Kenya agricultural incomes rose by 20 per cent from 1954–9 as compared with a 16
per cent rise in Tanganyika and a probable slight fall in Uganda.[12]

The improvement in Kenya African farming has come of
economic and political necessity, and even with its aid, the
African community continues to be a relatively underprivileged

TABLE 31

Kenya, Uganda, and Tanganyika: Exports in 1961 (by value)

	Total for the three territories per cent	Kenya per cent	Uganda per cent	Tanganyika per cent
Coffee	25.5	30.0	35.6	14.3
Cotton	19.6	1.8	42.7	14.4
Sisal	14.8	11.9	Nil	29.6
Tea	5.5	11.4	3.7	2.8
Hides and skins	3.4	4.4	2.0	3.7
Diamonds	4.7	Nil	Nil	12.0
Meat and meat preparations	3.5	6.5	Nil	4.3
Copper and alloy	2.8	1.5	7.5	Nil
Animal feeding stuffs	1.9	Nil	4.0	1.4
Oil seed	2.7	1.4	2.0	4.0
Pyrethrum and extract	2.5	8.7	Nil	*
Other	13.1	22.3	6.5	13.5
Total values	£121.8 mil	£35.2 mil	£39.2 mil	£47.4 mil

*Negligible.

SOURCES: *East African Economic and Statistical Review*, September 1962. *U.N. Yearbook of International Trade Statistics 1961*, pp. 384, 611, and 645.

group in Kenya. Purchasing power is still much more concentrated in the non-African communities than is the case in the other territories.[13]

In Tanganyika, as in Kenya, a high proportion of the export production is still in non-African hands. Sisal on large plantations in the Tanga area, coffee and tea in the highland regions. There is, however, a much greater proportion of African export production than in Kenya, notably of coffee around Mt Kilimanjaro and cotton and coffee from the southern end of Lake Victoria.

Both Kenya and Tanganyika have a greater variety of export crops than some African countries, which makes a lowering of price in any one commodity easier to bear. Uganda, however, is much too dependent on two African-grown crops, coffee and cotton, which together account for over 80 per cent of total exports by value.

Coffee is the most profitable for the farmer but is mostly of the low-grade *robusta* type (in contrast to Kenya *arabica*) and hard to sell in a coffee-glutted world market. Cotton pays the farmer less but has a more ready sale in the world market. In the case of both crops, output per man is too low and the increased production of recent years has largely come from taking more land into cultivation.

Uganda is more fortunate than her neighbours in having more land available which is suitable for arable farming. Indeed this may be one reason for the low farming standards in most of the country. The land and the climate are sufficiently good to support a relatively dense population at the subsistence level. There has been less of a challenge for survival than in Kenya and the tentative entry of most farmers into the money economy still has an air of incompleteness about it. Most farmers still have a bigger stake in subsistence agriculture than in commercial farming.

Mining has been developed in all three territories in so far as resources are known and transport available to tap them. Copper mining in Uganda had to wait on the completion of the western railway extension. Diamonds from Mwadui provide an increasing proportion of Tanganyika's export revenue while Kenya, the poorest of the three in minerals, has developed the mining of soda.

Tanganyika has extensive reserves of coal and iron in the south-west but they are remote from communications and population centres and unlikely to be worked in the near future. Industrial development is in its infancy in all three territories although Kenya now makes a wide range of consumer goods including shoes, processed foods, window frames, and glassware.

The difficulty of attracting industry to Uganda illustrates the major economic problem of East Africa as a whole; the raising of farm output and thus of purchasing power to stimulate local demand. When the government built the Owen Falls dam at Jinja to provide hydro-electricity, it was expected that spontaneous industrial growth would follow. In fact this did not happen. Electricity made possible a textile mill, a cement factory, and a copper smelter, but there was no rush from other industrial users. Indeed it has been said that 'hydro-electricity appears to have done more to brighten up the town at night, and to make life pleasanter for the better-off sections of the population than to promote industrial growth.'[14] Without an increasing local market there is little likelihood of further industrial expansion. The raising of farm output and farm incomes remains the first priority.

THE EAST AFRICAN COMMON SERVICES ORGANIZATION

This organization was set up in 1947 as the E.A. High Comission, to administer certain common services throughout British East Africa. There are the so-called 'self-contained' (i.e. self-financing) services like railways, ports, posts and telecommunications, and the 'non self-contained' services like research, meteorology, and higher education, to which all the territories contribute. With independence coming at different times in the different countries, the continued existence of these common services has presented a serious political problem.

Kenya, Uganda, and Tanganyika each participate in the E.A.C.S.O. For the time being all the common services will continue and the common tariff against the outside world will be maintained. The question as yet undecided is the long-term future of the organization – will it be strengthened or will it succumb to increasing economic nationalism on the part of the three territories?

It is clear that each country has benefited from the common economic links. Kenya has gained a market of over twenty million people for her manufactured goods and dairy products, Uganda has an assured outlet to the sea over which it has its share of control, while Tanganyika, like the others, can draw on the services of the organization's skilled personnel.

These are assets which none of the countries can afford to lose. They will be unique in Africa if they survive the transition to independence and could provide the basis for closer economic and political integration in the future. In this they are like the arrangements which the Common Market countries have made in Europe.

All the East African countries are committed to a political federation, but it has proved difficult to implement this intention in practice. The only definite political union so far is the United Republic of Tanganyika and Zanzibar (Now renamed Tanzania).

When the High Commission was set up it was proposed that certain items should be included in the Commission's powers which were in fact excluded in the final agreement. These included things like industrial licensing and commercial legislation. They would not only have meant considerably more control over economic planning but also the giving up of more sovereignty than the territorial governments were willing to consider.

If the Common Services Organization was now strengthened on the lines originally proposed in 1947 it could *evolve* into a federal authority without any painful political decision being taken by those who are now reluctant. The history of rapid political federation in Africa has not been a happy one. Both Mali (Soudan-Senegal) and the United Arab Republic (Egypt-Syria) have ceased to exist, as has the Central African Federation. East Africa has the framework of a different and slower road to unity. It may, however, be more lasting if the goal is clear and the will to co-operate maintained. There is, at any rate, a unique opportunity to try.

ZANZIBAR

The islands of Zanzibar and Pemba were once the centre of trade and civilization on the east African coast. In the mid-nineteenth century in particular, under the reign of Sultan Seyyid Said and his successors, Zanzibar became the commercial centre of the area with a flourishing trade in slaves and ivory. It is estimated that Zanzibar had an annual import of some 15,000 slaves during the first half of the nineteenth century.[15] Today the islands rely almost exclusively on the production and export of cloves and clove oil. In 1959 they formed 74 per cent of exports by value, the remainder consisting of coconuts and coconut products. About half the trade in cloves is with Indonesia and a third with India.[16]

The total population is about 300,000 of whom 76.5 per cent are classified as Africans and 15.7 per cent Arabs.[17] Traditionally the islands have been ruled by the Arabs, and the Zanzibar Nationalist Party, controlled by the Arab minority, still had a bare majority of seats in the legislature until the 1964 revolution. Zanzibar has now given up its sovereignty to join with Tanganyika in a United Republic (Tanzania).

RUANDA AND BURUNDI

These two countries were formerly parts of German East Africa which have, since 1919, been administered by Belgium under League of Nations Mandate and U.N. Trusteeship. Both are densely populated agricultural countries with a rapidly increasing population and an acute shortage of agricultural land.

Most of the population is concerned mainly with subsistence agriculture, but there has been increasing attention paid in recent years to the growing of cash crops, especially coffee and cotton. Some tin is mined but the immediate prospects of mineral development are not considered good. Situated over 1,000 miles from the sea, with poorly developed communications with the outside world, Ruanda and Burundi have been less developed economically than neighbouring countries and there has been a considerable outflow of labour to Uganda and to the mines of Katanga.

In both Ruanda and Burundi about 15 per cent of the population are Tutsi and about 85 per cent are Hutu. There are also a few Twa pygmoid hunters. The Tutsi are pastoralists who entered the country between the fifteenth and the eighteenth century and who were able to subdue the more numerous agricultural Hutu.

Until recently this Tutsi rule has been maintained, but in Ruanda the Hutu, through their party, PARMEHUTU, and the support of the Belgian administration, have been able to depose the Tutsi king and to remove most of the Tutsi from positions of power. This revolution has been accompanied by much violence and the outflow of refugees in their thousands to neighbouring Uganda, Tanganyika, and Congo (Leopoldville).

In Burundi, recent events have been far more peaceful. The monarchy is more firmly established and there has been less friction between Tutsi and Hutu. In the 1961 elections the anti-

Belgian UPRONA party was elected with an overwhelming majority and in spite of the subsequent assassination of its leader there has so far been no communal strife in Burundi.

It seems likely, therefore, that Ruanda and Burundi may tread different political paths in the future. It is at least possible that Burundi will rejoin with Tanganyika while the state of near civil war in Ruanda makes the future there extremely uncertain. We shall almost certainly, however, have to forget the term 'Ruanda-Urundi' and think instead of Ruanda and Burundi as political units separate from each other.* This is not really surprising when viewed in historical perspective.

A series of Hamitic kingdoms, including Ruanda and Urundi, were established in Central Africa, probably in the eighteenth century. These kingdoms, despite their common origins, were constantly at war with one another. The kings of Ruanda and Urundi were almost always enemies ... When the Europeans occupied the country they found two absolute monarchies, separate and distinct, each headed by a king, each with its own organization and its own language. . . . There is still very little contact between the indigenous authorities of Ruanda and Urundi, and their respective populations are still kept apart by their traditional particularism. Thus the administration had to abandon in 1951-2, because of the opposition of the people, a scheme to standardize the spelling of Kirundi and Kinyaruanda, languages which are so closely related as to call for assimilation if not complete fusion.[18]

*Achieved independence as two independent states, July 1962.

Notes on Chapter 11

1. *East Africa Royal Commission 1953–5 Report*, pp. 256–7. Tsetse fly is on the increase in parts of Uganda.
2. Even this possibility is limited. In the *Economic Development of Tanganyika* it is said that, 'A rough calculation suggests that around 4 million acres could be opened up for crop production by irrigation or flood control. This is less than 2 per cent of the total area of the territory . . .'
Report of a Mission organized by the International Bank for Reconstruction and Development, 1961, p. 18.
3. *E. A. Royal Commission Report*, p. 279.
4. J. E. Goldthorpe, *Outlines of East African Society*, 1959, p. 40. (Photolithographed and published by Dept. of Sociology, Makerere University College.) This book is an excellent summary and analysis of available information on east African society, though now somewhat dated.
5. *Board of Trade Journal*, 25 August 1961. Special article on 'Exporting to East Africa', p. 19.
6. Report of the Uganda Relationships Commission 1961 (*The Munster Report*), p. 89.
7. Colonial Office *Annual Report, Part II*, p. 9.
8. See especially E. Huxley, *White Man's Country*, 1935, for one important source of the myth.
9. The chief exception is the Goan Roman Catholic Group.
10. *Tanganyika*. Colonial Office *Annual Report*, 1960.
Kenya Statistical Abstract, 1960.
Uganda Census, 1959. 'Non-African population'.
11. op. cit., p. 65.
See also L. W. Hollingsworth, *The Asians of East Africa*, 1960.
12. *East Africa, Report of the Economic and Fiscal Commission* 1961, p. 21 (H.M.S.O.Cmd 1279).

13. *Board of Trade Journal*, op. cit., p. 21.
14. W. Elkan, *The Economic Development of Uganda*, Oxford University Press, 1961, p. 60.
15. Hollingsworth, op. cit., p. 28.
16. C.O. 'Report', 1959.
17. Central Office of Information Fact Sheets on U.K. Dependencies: Zanzibar 1961.
18. U.N. Report on Ruanda-Urundi, 1957, p. 14.
    See also:
    S. J. Baker, 'The Distribution of the Native Population over East Africa', *Africa*, Vol. 10, 1937.
    J. Huxley, *Africa View*, Chatto, 1931 – inevitably dated but still worth reading.
    N. Leys, *Kenya*, 1924, for an early attack on land alienation. Well documented.

Southern Africa
12 The Republic of South Africa, Bechuanaland, Basutoland, and Swaziland

With the most developed economy, abundant resources, and the highest income per head in all Africa, the Republic might in some circumstances appear to be the most favoured country in the continent. But because it also has the most acute racial problems, it is probably the continent's unhappiest country instead. It is certainly the most modern – both in terms of economic development and of settlement.

THE PEOPLE

Prior to European settlement in the Cape during the seventeenth century, the Western half of the Cape Province was sparsely inhabited by Bushmen hunters and Khoi-Khoin (Hottentot) pastoralists, most of whom were either exterminated or have since been absorbed into the Cape Coloured population.[1] The eastern half of Cape Province and the whole of the coastlands of Natal had been settled for many centuries by Bantu-speaking people. At the time of the European advance eastwards in the eighteenth century, the south-westward frontier of the Bantu lay approximately along the line of the Great Fish river. This line was the first point of violent conflict between Boer and Bantu and it is important to remember its location for two reasons. First, in any discussion of 'historic rights' between the two groups, the Boers can claim they were first only in the western half of the Cape Province, not in the rest of the country. Second, all the Bantu areas (or 'Native Reserves' as they used to be called) are in the north and east.

The bare numbers and percentages in Table 32 do not give a clear picture of the distribution of the various groups, and the figures should be read in conjunction with the distribution on Map 26. The most significant facts which emerge from this are

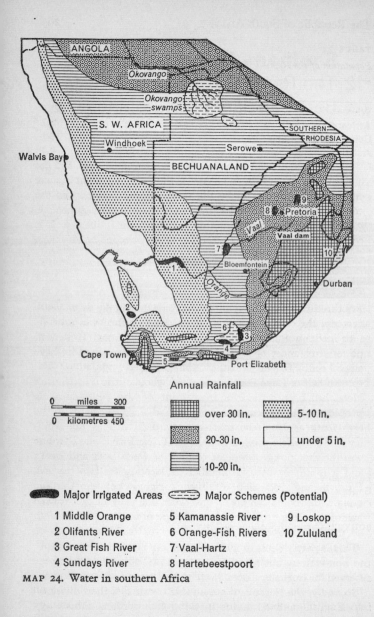

Annual Rainfall

▦	over 30 in.	⠿	5-10 in.
▨	20-30 in.	☐	under 5 in.
▤	10-20 in.		

◖◗ Major Irrigated Areas ⊂⊃ Major Schemes (Potential)

1 Middle Orange   5 Kamanassie River   9 Loskop
2 Olifants River   6 Orange-Fish Rivers   10 Zululand
3 Great Fish River   7 Vaal-Hartz
4 Sundays River   8 Hartebeestpoort

MAP 24. Water in southern Africa

TABLE 32

Population of the Republic by race (1957 estimate)

		per cent
Whites	2,957,000	20.9
Africans	9,460,000	66.7
Coloureds (including Cape Malays)	1,319,000	9.1
Asiatics	431,000	3.3
	14,167,000	100.0

SOURCE: 'State of the Union' *Yearbook for South Africa 1958.*

that there are comparatively few Africans (Bantu) in the Western Cape (where their place is taken by the Coloureds), and that most of the Indians (Asiatics) live in Natal.[2] There is, too, a difference in racial composition between town and country which we will deal with later.

The Europeans of South Africa are unique in Africa for at least three reasons. First, there are many more of them than anywhere else on the continent, so that they cannot be dismissed as an insignificant minority. They amount to more than one fifth of the total population and not only exercise complete political control over the rest, but do most of the jobs which can be classified as skilled.

TABLE 33

South Africa: Manual Workers in Industry (1946)

	Skilled per cent	Semi-skilled per cent	Unskilled per cent
Europeans	85	30	1
Bantu	5	40	85
Others	10	30	14

SOURCE: *Census of Population, Union of S. Africa 1946.*

This is partly because most of them are better educated than the non-whites, but also because most of the skilled jobs are reserved for Europeans only, both by legislation and by tradition.

Secondly, the Europeans are unique because of their division into English- and Afrikaans-speaking communities. About 45

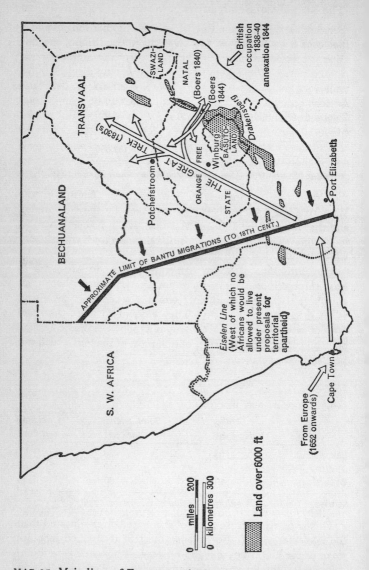

MAP 25. Main lines of European colonization in South Africa up to
the middle of the 19th century

per cent of Whites have English as their mother tongue and 55 per cent have Afrikaans. For most people in Britain, the Boer War is a remote piece of history, but for white South Africans the memories of this, and other conflicts among themselves, are still very much alive. In spite of the Act of Union of 1909, which brought together the two communities in political independence, they are far from united over many fundamental issues – attitudes to law, democracy, religion and, to some extent, race relations among the most important.

Finally, the Europeans are unique because of their long history in Africa. Most other European 'settlers' in Africa are newcomers in this century. White South Africans, and especially the Afrikaners, can look back to 300 years of history *in Africa*. South Africa is more home to them than any European country.*

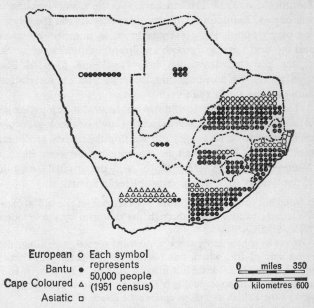

European o Each symbol
Bantu • represents
Cape Coloured △ 50,000 people
Asiatic □ (1951 census)

0   miles   350
0   kilometres   600

MAP 26. Southern Africa: distribution of population by region and race. (From J. D. Fage, *An Atlas of African History*, 1958, p. 51)

By 1795 there were about 16,000 settlers[3] and it is from these

*See Chapter 3, p. 59.

people that the Republic's Afrikaners are descended. Permanent British occupation of the Cape only came in 1806.

With the advent of British rule there was increasing discontent among the Boer farmers. They felt that their identity was threatened and they were unsympathetic to the more liberal native policy of the Cape government. Such was their discontent that they decided to leave the Cape altogether and to undertake in the 1830s the Great Trek north to the high veld, to establish what later became the independent Boer republics of the Orange Free State and the Transvaal.

The Great Trek involved at least 10,000 people, moving across 500 miles of mountain and plateau in convoys of ox wagons. To the east the way was barred by the human barrier of Bantu tribesmen and the physical barrier of the mountains of Basutoland and the Drakensberg. To the north-west the land was dry and uninviting. Only to the north-east was the way open, the native population greatly reduced in numbers by warfare, and the land suitable for both arable and pastoral farming. Some of the pioneers descended into Natal and founded Pietermaritzburg, but numbers migrated again on the annexation of Natal by Britain in 1844.

The Boer farmers settled down on the veld to enjoy their hard-won independence, preserving their Calvinist theology, evolving their own special language, and treating the natives according to their lights. 'There shall be no equality between Black and White either in Church or State,' said the original constitution of the Transvaal. Their present belief in apartheid

is based not simply on fear of the African, but on the will to preserve the culture handed down through the centuries by the founders of White South Africa.

It seems a bare inheritance, an inward-turned, unsmiling, dourly pious way of life, which has never flowered notably in literature, music, or the visual arts; but it has a kind of bleak dignity, and the story of the Afrikaner people is the story of a long fight to protect it against the British as well as against the Bantu.[4]

English-speaking white South Africans are of more recent origins, since many of them came after 1860 with the development of first diamond and then gold mining. Before this, settlers had been brought into the Cape in the 1820s and again in the

1840s and '50s – probably about 22,000 in all. In the same period (up to 1856) about 8,000 Europeans had settled in Natal.

Immigration on a large scale – mainly British – followed on the discovery of diamonds in the Cape and gold in the Transvaal. It was a development the Afrikaners did not welcome but could not stop. No accurate figures exist of immigration at this time, but some indication is given in the growth of the white population (from all sources) in Transvaal between 1890 and 1911 – from 119,000 to 421,000. This influx of '*Uitlanders*' has had its effect on the linguistic balance between town and country even today. Until very recently English has been predominant in the towns (especially in the newer industrial centres) and Afrikaans in the countryside, and although Afrikaners have joined the townward movement in recent years, they remain rooted in 'pre-industrial Europe. The English section arrived after the industrial revolution which had transformed the country of their birth. They brought with them the modern ideas of commerce and finance . . .'[5] This urban dominance of the English-speaking Whites has meant that although the Afrikaners have for long been dominant in politics, they have until recently been under-represented in the professions (including the judiciary) and even more under-represented in business enterprises.[6]

The Coloureds are of exceedingly mixed racial origin and, like the Afrikaners, their roots go back to the early days of settlement at the Cape. 89 per cent of them still live in the Cape Province, and 60 per cent have Afrikaans as their mother tongue.

Their ancestors include Bushmen, Hottentots, Europeans, slaves (of Malayan, West African, Malagasy, or Indian origin among others) and passing sailors of all races. Offspring of European-Hottentot unions have sometimes preserved a special identity and are known as Bastards; one of the best known groups are the Rehoboth Bastards of South-West Africa. Only the Cape Malays have preserved their racial and cultural distinctiveness, due to the social cohesion which the practice of Islam has given them. They number today about 65,000 people.

The formation of the Coloured community has been a continuing process right up until the present time. Between 1937 and 1946 there were, on average, about 700 'mixed' marriages annually,[7] apart from other less permanent unions; although, with the application of apartheid legislation, this process will no doubt decrease. There has, moreover, been a continuing traffic *from* the Coloured people of those whose physical make-up enabled them to 'play white'. Nobody knows how many have been absorbed into the White population or how many 'Whites' carry Coloured genes. Certainly many Whites must be partly Coloured, and one writer has estimated their number as at least half a million.[8]

The Asians are descended from indentured labourers brought over from India to work in the sugar plantations of Natal, and most of them still live in that province – over half in the city of Durban alone. Many have risen to wealth and influence there, although the majority are still poor. It has long been the dream of the Whites that the Indians would one day be repatriated to India. A state-assisted scheme has been in force since 1927, but the numbers taking advantage of it have never been great. Since the Second World War less than a thousand Indians have accepted this Government assistance.

The Bantu tribes had moved into the eastern half of South Africa from the north some centuries before White settlement at the Cape. Like the Whites, they displaced, absorbed, or destroyed what indigenous inhabitants were already living there.

Although 'Bantu' is really a linguistic not a racial term, the South African Bantu do have a different appearance from the Negroes of West Africa. For example, they are of lighter skin colour, probably due to admixture with the yellow-skinned Hottentot and Bushmen. This relatively light skin colour is particularly noticeable among the Xhosa, some of whom have been known to 'play Coloured' in the same way that Coloureds have played white.

The two main groups of Bantu languages in South Africa are the Nguni and the Sotho. These are further sub-divided according to the following table, which also gives the approximate percentage of Bantu which speak them.

TABLE 34

Bantu Languages in the Republic and the High Commission Territories

		per cent
Nguni Group	Xhosa	32
	Zulu including Ndebele	30
	Swazi	3
	Tsonga	3
	Venda	2
Sotho Group	S. Sotho	10
	N. Sotho	10
	Tswana	8
	Other	2

SOURCE: *Tomlinson Commission Report.*

It will be seen that the main groups of importance (roughly one third each) are the Xhosa, Zulu and Sotho, but it should be remembered that some of the urban Bantu know no tribal language. The Drakensberg mountains form the boundary between the Sotho and the Nguni groups in the same way that they formed the boundary between Briton and Boer in the nineteenth century. They also form a climatic divide at all times and are still a barrier to communications.

The Africans are the least urbanized of the South African peoples but they have been moving into the urban areas in ever increasing numbers during this century. In 1904 only 10.4 per cent of Bantu were town dwellers while, by 1951, 27.1 per cent lived in the urban areas – two thirds of these in the four main industrial centres,[9] where they congregate in shanty towns and 'locations' surrounding the White cities. The explosive social and political problems created by these urban Africans are the chief focuses of race tensions in the Republic.

TABLE 35

Percentage of Population Living in the Urban Areas of South Africa
(1951)

	per cent
Total	42.6
Europeans	78.4
Asiatics	77.5
Coloureds	64.4
Africans	27.1

SOURCE: *Census of Population, Union of South Africa* (1951).

THE LAND AND ITS RESOURCES

As anyone knows who reads the travel posters or the labels at the fruiterers, South Africa is a land of sunshine as well as race tensions. Although much of the north and west is too dry for arable farming, the country has a great deal of good agricultural land, abundant mineral resources, no tsetse fly (except in part of Northern Natal) and a climate over most of the country which is generally regarded as invigorating for human activity.

The two main regions of commercial arable farming are those which have more than 20 inches of rainfall as well as a temperate climate. They are the area around Cape Town and the High Veld (most of Orange Free State and Southern Transvaal) and contain the chief concentrations of white farmers. A third region of commercial arable farming is the coastal strip of Natal, specializing in sugar cane and to a lesser extent bananas and other tropical fruits.

The Western Cape region, having a Mediterranean type of climate with good winter rain and hot dry summers, specializes in wheat, vines (both for dessert and wine making) and in temperate fruits like apples, pears, and peaches. Fruit in particular has found a ready market in the northern hemisphere, where it appears in the off-season for home-grown fruit. This off-season peak in marketing in Europe probably accounts for the material (as distinct from propaganda) failure of the boycott of March 1960 in Britain. In many shops it would be a case of buying South African or going without.

The Western Cape region of winter rain merges gradually along the coast into the summer rainfall region of the eastern half of the country. Animal husbandry as well as arable farming becomes important, and there is some citrus fruit growing, especially in the irrigated areas north of Port Elizabeth.

The High Veld at an elevation of from 4,000 to 6,000 ft lies to the west of the Drakensberg mountains. It is naturally a region of rolling grassy plain – the *platteland* (flat land) home of the Afrikaner nation. At the centre of the region is the so-called 'maize triangle', containing some three quarters of the Republic's cultivated area. Although this is the centre of maize growing in the Republic it is by no means confined to this area, nor is the region entirely dominated by the cultivation of maize. It is essentially a land of mixed arable and pastoral farming. To the north, in the lower-lying and warmer Bush Veld of the central and northern Transvaal, tobacco and citrus fruits become important.

In over half of South Africa 'the spectre that haunts the farmer most frequently is drought. Some 53 per cent of the Union has an average rainfall of less than 20 inches and the variability of this rainfall . . . tends to be proportionately greater as the mean amount decreases.'[10] In these drier areas, in the centre and west of the country, the dominant activity is cattle and even more sheep farming of an extensive kind – extensive in the sense that animals (and men) are scattered over a wide area of sparse pasture. The absence of the tsetse fly has aided this development. There are in South Africa over eleven million head of cattle and over thirty-one million sheep, compared with 5½ million cattle and four million sheep in the whole of the Central African Federation, S. W. Africa, Bechuanaland and Moçambique combined. In 1951 wool came second to gold in South Africa's exports (£91 million). This underlines still further the difficulty of organizing a consumer boycott of South African goods. Fruit and wine may be fairly easy to identify: wool is not.

The conservation of available water supplies is important not only for agriculture but also for industry and the needs of a growing urban population moving rapidly towards Western standards of consumption. This is particularly significant on the Witwatersrand, which draws most of its water from wells and from the Vaal dam at Vereeniging. In 1947, 67½ million gallons of water per day were used on the Rand (about half by industry and the mines) but by A.D. 2000 it is estimated that 953 million gallons will be required. More dams will certainly be needed to cope with this demand and with the needs of agriculture. The trouble is that the Republic's rivers, being shallow and irregular in flow, are not well suited for the construction of dams and irrigation schemes. The major irrigated areas and potential schemes are indicated on Map 24.

South Africa lies at the southern end of

... the richest mineral belt so far discovered on the earth's surface, stretching from Katanga and the Northern Rhodesian Copperbelt in the north ... to the northern Cape Province ... No other area of comparable size can show so large and so continuous an output of gold, diamonds, copper, coal, iron, chrome, manganese, asbestos and ... uranium.[11]

All of these the Republic has in abundance. It is particularly fortunate in having by far the largest reserves of bituminous coal in the whole of Africa. Whereas it has less opportunity than many other African countries for the development of hydro-electric power, it also has less need.*

The development of gold and diamond mining in the 1870s brought the first large-scale foreign investment to South Africa. It upset the quiet pastoral life of the Boer farmers but it also provided the basis of capital and labour for later economic growth. It was thought at one time that the problem of finding a sufficient number of workers able and willing to work in the mines of the Rand might be solved by bringing in Chinese labour, and there were in fact some 55,000 Chinese there in the early years of this century. However, these were all repatriated by 1910 and the mines have since had to rely on the recruitment of Africans over an extensive area of southern Africa. This migrant labour is housed in special compounds near the mines, and workers usually come under contract for a spell of fourteen months or so before returning to their homes elsewhere in the

*But there is no oil – a fact of some importance if an economic boycott of South Africa ever became a reality.

Republic or in Moçambique, Central Africa and the High Commission Territories. The mine compounds are under the control of the Mining Companies and should not be confused with the shanty towns and 'locations' elsewhere on the Rand, which are under the control of the municipal authorities.

Iron and steel form the basis of modern manufacturing industry, and the beginnings were made in South Africa during the First World War. It was not until the formation of the South African Iron and Steel Corporation in 1928, however, that a firm basis was laid for the development of the Union into a modern industrial state. The Corporation (I.S.C.O.R.) established a works at Pretoria in 1934, using local ore, but the most spectacular development came in the 1950s with the beginnings of operations at the new, fully integrated steelworks at Vanderbijl Park near Vereeniging. This works, which comprises coke ovens, blast furnaces, slab, strip, and rolling mills, and ancillary plants for by-products, came into operation in 1951 and now has an ingot capacity of over 2 million tons. What in 1948 was a piece of open veld now contains a township of nearly 50,000 people, besides all the industrial plant. Ore is obtained from Thabazimbi in the western Transvaal and also from Sishen in the north-western Cape. Coal comes from the Newcastle area of Natal and from Witbank. I.S.C.O.R., a Government-owned enterprise, produces about two thirds of South Africa's steel requirements.

TABLE 36

Growth of Steel Production in South Africa

	(in thousands of metric tons)
1948	651
1954	1197
1955	1301
1956	1356
1957	1419
1958	1582
1959	1807
1960	2000
1961	2328

SOURCE: *U.N Statistical Yearbook 1962*, p. 256.

THE GROWTH OF SECONDARY INDUSTRY

Investment in mining, the growth of an urban labour force, Government encouragement and protection and, especially, the stimulus given by the Second World War have brought about an industrial revolution in the Republic in recent years. This has taken place above all on the Witwatersrand and to a lesser extent in the three other major industrial centres of Durban, Port Elizabeth/Uitenhage and Cape Town. 83.7 per cent of the net output of secondary industry in 1951 was concentrated in these four centres, 45.9 per cent in the southern Transvaal alone. In 1951, 32.1 per cent of the total population of South Africa was contained in the four areas – 55.4 per cent of the Whites and 21.4 per cent of the Africans. One third of the Whites and nearly one sixth of the Africans were concentrated in the southern Transvaal alone.

In the Cape Town area the main industries are clothing and textiles, canning and food processing, distilling, printing, and leather working. Port Elizabeth is the centre of the Republic's footwear industry and also has plants for car assembly, tyres, batteries, and food canning and processing. Durban concentrates on chemicals, paints, paper, hardware, clothing, and domestic appliances, while the southern Transvaal is the centre of the country's metal-working and engineering industries, among others.

This industrial growth has been accompanied by an influx of workers – both white and non-white – from the countryside. It has affected the balance between town and country and also between the various racial groups in different areas. Africans have left the reserves in larger numbers than ever before but Whites too have left their traditional strongholds. 'The migration of Whites is proportionately greater than any group except for the Asiatics.'[12] Huge areas of the Republic have far smaller white populations today than they had forty years ago. Not only in the countryside has this shrinkage of white South Africa been apparent. In 1957 Cape Town, Port Elizabeth, Pretoria, and Pietermaritzburg were the only towns in which Whites outnumbered Africans, while Pretoria is the only town in which the Whites are still more numerous than all other groups combined.

Industrialization has not only brought the different racial groups into greater geographical proximity, but has had the effect of breaking down barriers within industry. Gone are the days of the 1920s when the first Hertzog Government introduced discriminatory legislation to protect the interests of poor white workers. The industrial expansion has brought about a shortage of labour and as a result Bantu have been moving into the skilled and semi-skilled jobs. As early as 1946 nearly half the semi-skilled jobs were being done by Africans. If there are not enough white men to do the jobs available, black men will be asked to do them. By 1948 the process of industrial growth had not brought greater social and political rights for Africans, but it had improved their purchasing power as well as enhanced their importance in the economy of the country. It had, above all, centralized social and political pressures in the key industrial areas, particularly the southern Transvaal. Left unchecked it might well have brought about closer integration of the various racial groups. It was this possibility that the Nationalist Government, coming to power in 1948, at once tried to prevent from happening.

They argue that there are two courses open to South Africa. Either the process of integration can be allowed to continue, in which case eventual cultural and social equality will lead to complete racial assimilation: or, as this is too horrible to contemplate for them, the races must be kept apart in all spheres. To this end they have passed, and have started to put into effect, a whole complex of legislation designed to prevent any sort of contact whatever (except the master-servant relationship) between the different racial groups.

THE GEOGRAPHY OF APARTHEID

The Bantu are to have political and other rights of citizenship only in the Bantu Areas, i.e. in the present native reserves. In the White areas they will be allowed to work, but not to have permanent homes. In these areas they have to live in segregated townships and within these townships each person is classified according to his tribal origin so that he will be made to feel that his first loyalty is to the tribe and not to the urban community.

Above all, an attempt is to be made to decentralize industrial growth so that expansion in the four main nuclei can be slowed down and industries started on the fringes of the reserves. To encourage fewer Bantu to leave the reserves, economic development will be encouraged within the Bantu areas themselves. The blueprint for this geographical apartheid is known as the *Tomlinson Report* and was issued in the form of an extended summary in 1955.[13]

The present Bantu areas consist of rather less than 13 per cent of the total area of South Africa, situated in the form of a horseshoe around the Transvaal and Orange Free State. They are excessively fragmented. (See Map 27.)

The horseshoe shape of the Bantu areas and to some extent their fragmentation into many separate blocks can be explained by the historical geography ... The Europeans who first moved eastwards along the coast clashed with a southward moving stream of Bantu in the region of the present Ciskei. As a result of these clashes and other circumstances, a very broken up Ciskei was produced, while a large northward movement of Europeans occurred which took the form of the Great Trek ... the Europeans found little difficulty in establishing themselves on the grassy plains of the Orange Free State and the Transvaal.[14]

The Bantu were already settled in the warmer bushveld areas.

The reserves in the south-east are well watered and have a relatively high density of population (82 per sq. ml.). Those in the west are semi-desert areas with a much lower density of population (25 per sq. ml.), while those in the north are well watered tropical and sub-tropical areas with a density of 57 to the square mile. Apart from the cities of the White areas, the reserves in the north and south-east are the most densely populated parts of the country.

All the Bantu areas are run-down rural areas of subsistence agriculture, concentrating on the cultivation of 'mealies' (maize) and 'kaffircorn' (sorghum). There are no industries, nor any towns or cities. The whole of the population lives in villages of varying size. Even the larger villages (such as Umtata in the Transkei) do not have the range of services and amenities associated with towns in the real sense of the word. In general,

MAP 27. Lines of European development in relation to the Bantu areas as proposed by the Tomlinson Commission

the main lines of communication have left them on one side. A place like Port St Johns, which figures prominently on atlas maps, is described as 'unfortunately silted up to such an extent ... as to become unusable'[15]. Soil erosion is widespread.

In the Transkei, for example, 30 per cent of the land is badly eroded, 44 per cent moderately so, while only 26 per cent is free from erosion (but may be too hilly for cultivation). In consequence of this and of primitive farming methods, productivity is extremely low. In short, the reserves are completely under-developed backward areas within the boundaries of what is, in some parts, a modern industrial state.

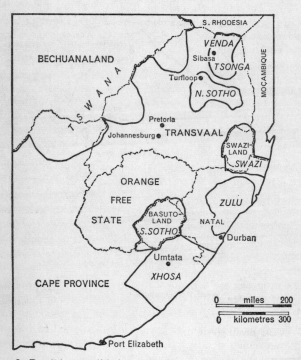

MAP 28. Possible consolidation of the Bantu areas as proposed by the Tomlinson Commission

At present some 42.6 per cent[16] of the Bantu live in the reserves, and the density of population has certainly reached beyond the upper limits of their capacity without extensive development. The Tomlinson Report suggests that by the year 2000 the racial balance of South Africa's population will be as follows:

Whites	4,588,000
Bantu	21,361,000
Coloureds	3,917,000
Asiatics	1,382,000

It argues, moreover, that,

If the tempo of urbanization experienced during 1946–51 is continued to the close of the century . . . then more than 10,000,000 Bantu will be established in urban areas . . . Moreover if the present absorbent capacity of the Bantu areas, European farms and other rural areas is not raised . . . more than 15,000,000 of the above mentioned 21 million Bantu will be living in the urban areas outside the Bantu areas. . . . Unless economic development can be diverted from its present geographical concentration . . . it may be anticipated also that the vast majority of these Bantu will be concentrated at the four existing industrial complexes . . .[17]

The report therefore suggests that an effort should be made to divert European industries to the fringes of the reserves,[18] to which Bantu labour can travel daily, and that the reserves themselves should be developed extensively both industrially and agriculturally. To this end it makes detailed proposals involving among other things the creation of a development authority and the expenditure of £104 millions in the first ten years.

The proposals are dependent on the incorporation into South Africa of the three High Commission Territories of Bechuanaland, Basutoland, and Swaziland, and the suggestion is made that the areas might be consolidated as indicated in Map 28. After consolidation and incorporation the Bantu areas would amount to 47 per cent of 'Greater South Africa'.

If sufficient money is spent and if the Territories at present under British rule are acquired (however remote this possibility may be) then the report suggests that the Bantu areas could support a population of 8 million together with 1½ million dependent on work in White industries outside the reserves. If migratory labourers are added this would amount to a '*de jure*

population' of about 10 millions – about the same *proportion* as
are at present supported in the reserves. In other words, even in
its most generous and optimistic form, apartheid could not make
racial separation any more effective than at present.

So far, little has been done to implement the proposals of the
Tomlinson Commission. A Bantu Investment Corporation was
set up in 1959 but with only £½ million initial capital. The Bantu
Self Government Act of 1959 envisaged the establishment of the
seven national units but with no suggestion of consolidation.
'University' colleges have been set up for Zulu, Xhosa, and
Sotho – the latter at Turfloop, visited by Mr Macmillan in his
1960 tour. And there is now a 'Government' in the Transkei.

Meanwhile the growth of the urban African population continues. Between 1951 and 1957 the African population of
Johannesburg, Durban, Pretoria, Vanderbijl Park, Vereeniging,
and Port Elizabeth increased by a total of 144,752 as opposed to
a White increase of 90,946.[19] Moreover the list of new industrial
enterprises started or planned in 1956–7 still shows a heavy concentration in the four main areas. Much of South Africa's private industry is still financed by foreign capital. The Tomlinson
Commission and to a lesser extent the Government may be
willing to subordinate economic to doctrinal interests. Private
investors and especially foreign investors are not.

In the long run, industrial development based on a segregated
labour force is bound to be inefficient even if it provides cheap
labour in the short run. Overheads are greater for one thing –
the provison and maintenance of two, three, or even four washing, eating, and lavatory facilities for workpeople can be an
expensive business. Not to be able to promote according to
ability and to have to keep job segregation enforced will also
become increasingly inefficient as more Africans become used
to industrial processes. Finally, the proposals of the Tomlinson
Commission for overall economic planning based on apartheid
will cut across the economic interests of the country, which
need to be developed as a whole, not piecemeal. Mineral resources and possibilities for irrigation in northern Transvaal,
for example, overlap both White and Bantu areas. To develop
them in the most efficient way would tend towards integration,
not apartheid.

The reliance on private, and especially foreign capital is, therefore, most important when considering the practicability of geographical apartheid. Investors will usually look for greatest profitability rather than bow to purely political considerations. Taken together with the need to incorporate the High Commission Territories, the large amount of investment involved, and the incomplete nature of the proposed separation (even at its most optimistic), the conclusion is inescapable that geographical apartheid is unworkable, although this does not seem to have weakened the determination to make it work in some form or other. Perhaps one day the South African Government will face up to the minority report of Mr Bisschop, a member of the Tomlinson Commission. 'If in due course, it is found unpractical,' he said, 'and I greatly fear that it will be found to be so, progressive integration with its economic and political consequences will have to be accepted.'[20]

13 South West Africa and the Protectorates

SOUTH WEST AFRICA

South West Africa is not important for what it is but for what it symbolizes to the outside world. It is a vast country nearly as big as Nigeria and almost eight times the size of England and Wales, but most of it is desert (the Namib) or semi-desert (the Kalahari) and at present supports only about half a million people.

To the outside world it symbolizes the struggle between black and white in South Africa. Ruled by South Africa since 1918 its international status is in dispute between the U.N.O. and the South African Government. After the First World War, the country was handed over to South Africa to be administered as a League of Nations Mandate. It was, however, a different type of mandated territory from any other in that it was allowed to be administered as an integral portion of the administering power.

In 1946 South Africa asked the U.N. to be allowed to incorporate S.W. Africa. This request was refused and South Africa was asked to place the territory under the U.N. Trusteeship system. The U.N. claims to be the legal heir of the League. South Africa claims that the League has no legal successor and therefore, that it has no obligation to place S.W. Africa under Trusteeship. Deadlock between the U.N. and South Africa over the status of S.W. Africa continues down to the present time.

The coastal Namib desert is one of the most truly arid regions of the world. Known to the early explorers as the 'skeleton coast' and the 'coast of death', it would today be almost entirely uninhabited were it not for the rich diamond deposits found there which now produce the chief revenue of the country. The diamonds are found in easily worked surface deposits.

The eastern half of the country, bordering on Bechuanaland, is also largely uninhabited, although the Kalahari is not such a forbidding area as the Namib and does support a small population of Bushman hunters, who wander over large areas in search of game.

The chief areas of population coincide with the areas of highest rainfall. In the north, still under a system of indirect rule, are the tribal areas of the Ovambo and others. In the central highlands are the chief areas of white settlement and social conflict.

The northern tribal territories are some of the most backward and untouched in the whole of Africa. Here live about two thirds of the African population and over half the total population. Theirs is still a life of subsistence agriculture and cattle farming with no exports save that of labour to the south. The area contains some of the best watered country in the whole of S.W. Africa, but it is malarial and tsetse-infested, and little money has been spent on it. There are certainly possibilities for future development.

The central highlands, lying between 5,000 and 8,000 feet, have a fairly low rainfall and are unsuitable for crop cultivation. However, they contain some of the finest ranching country in the whole of Southern Africa, and it is this which has attracted the European settlers. Today most of them are Afrikaners, with some Germans and a smaller number of English-speaking South Africans.

South-West Africa was a German colony from 1890 until after the first world war. Before the coming of the Germans the native tribes of the central highlands appear to have been fairly prosperous cattle farmers. The chief groups were the Hottentots and the Hereros, a Bantu tribe. The early explorers spoke of 'countless herds of horned cattle'[21] and when the territory was annexed by Germany 'the Herero people must have possessed over 150,000 head of cattle'.[22]

This prosperity was soon destroyed. In just over ten years a tribe of over 80,000 people had been reduced to less than 15,000 impoverished refugees,[23] mainly by the ruthless and bloody suppression of the Herero revolt of 1904. As a German Colonial Office official put it, writing in 1890:

The decision to colonize in South-West Africa could after all mean nothing else but this; namely that the native tribes would have to give up their land in order that the white man might have the land ...
When this attitude is questioned from the moral law standpoint,

the answer is that for nations of the *Kultur* position of the South Africa natives, the loss of their free national barbarism and their development into a class of labourers in service of and dependent on the white people, is primarily a law of existence in the highest degree.[24]

Those who did not accept this doctrine had, quite naturally, to be suppressed.

During the inter-war years, S.W. Africa was an almost forgotten land. Annual reports were submitted to the League of Nations and although there was criticism of racial policies and lack of progress towards self-government, both reports and criticisms soon collected dust on the shelves of governments and publicists alike.

Since 1950 the South African government has unilaterally incorporated S.W. Africa into South Africa. S.W. African MPs sit in the South African Parliament and, as far as the central and southern areas are concerned, the territory is to all intents and purposes part of South Africa.

The U.N./South African dispute over the territory has grown more angry since 1946, but little progress has been made towards resolving it. The only suggestion for a compromise solution came from the 1958 U.N. Good Offices Committee under the chairmanship of Sir Charles Arden-Clarke. This suggestion was that the *status quo* should, in effect, be recognized and that the territory should be partitioned. The central and southern areas would become part of South Africa and the northern tribal areas made a separate territory and placed under U.N. Trusteeship.*

This suggestion for partition did not find much support in the Councils of the U.N. By this time the status of Africa had come to symbolize the whole quarrel between South Africa and most of the outside world over apartheid. Partition looked too much like a form of apartheid. In addition, the continued existence of the dispute provides the international opponents of apartheid with a legal weapon with which to fight South Africa. South Africa's racial policies are considered by some to be an 'internal affair' with which the U.N. is not competent to deal.

---

*The South African government has now accepted (1964) the Odendaal Commission Report. This recommends the establishment of ten 'Bantustans' and a white area – i.e. complete geographical apartheid.

S.W. Africa is an 'international' dispute and can, therefore, be used to provide a means of criticizing apartheid at the U.N. and, perhaps, acting against it as well. It is thus a far more significant country than its population, resources, and state of development alone would warrant.

BASUTOLAND, BECHUANALAND, AND SWAZILAND

These three British Protectorates are usually known as the High Commission Territories. They are administered, not by the Colonial Office, but by three Resident Commissioners responsible through a High Commissioner to the Commonwealth Relations Office. The High Commissioner is also the British Ambassador to the Republic (formerly Union) of South Africa.

Under the South Africa Act of 1909, which brought the Union into being, it was envisaged that the three territories might at some future date be incorporated into South Africa.[25] However, in spite of constant pressure from South Africa, Britain has continued to honour the pledge given in 1909, and renewed in 1959, that no transfer to South Africa would take place until the inhabitants had been consulted. It seems unthinkable that at the present time such a transfer could take place.

Bechuanaland is dependent economically on South Africa and its administrative headquarters was at Mafeking inside the Republic until recently.

It is a large country, some three times the size of the United Kingdom but supporting only about 340,000 people. Like S.W. Africa it is an arid land with a rainfall which varies from 12 inches in the west to 19 inches in the east.

The country can be divided into three natural regions. The Kalahari 'desert', better described as sand veld, for it provides some good seasonal grazing which could be extended; the Okovango Basin; and the relatively fertile and developed eastern strip near the railway line.

The Okovango Basin has been the subject of several inquiries and surveys. There are clearly large reserves of untapped water there, but the area is tsetse-infested and malarial, and no agreed scheme for the use of the Okovango water has yet been devised. Probably the Okovango Basin itself could be developed for agriculture and surplus water made available by canal for areas to the east.[26]

The eastern strip, near the railway, was the area which first interested Britain and contains about 80 per cent of the population. At the time a Protectorate was proclaimed (1895) it was regarded simply as a 'road into the interior',[27] a convenient by-pass for Rhodes' pioneers which would avoid the Transvaal and provide a clear line of expansion for the British empire in central Africa. Some of this eastern strip has been alienated to European farmers and there is a small area of European farming at Ghanzi, near the border of S.W. Africa.

Cattle farming is the most important economic activity and provides 75 per cent (by value) of total exports. The chief markets are in South Africa, the Congo, Rhodesia, but in 1958 some meat was, for the first time, exported overseas. Up until 1954 all cattle were exported on the hoof, but since then the abattoir at Lobatsi has been established and now takes about 90 per cent of the cattle exported.

Bechuanaland has workable coal reserves near the railway which could be used for power stations for the development of industry, and as an export to neighbouring countries. Before this is done, however, it is probably more important to improve the cattle industry, particularly by the better management of pastures, control of water supplies, and selective breeding. Together with improved communications to western areas, this could provide a firmer basis than at present on which future economic growth can rest.

Basutoland is entirely surrounded by South Africa and is the poorest of the three High Commission Territories. About two thirds of the country consists of high mountains rising to 11,000 ft and most of the population of about 700,000 is concentrated in the western lowlands.

The economy is almost entirely devoted to subsistence agriculture and the density of population in the more fertile areas has been accompanied by serious soil erosion. At present the only significant export is labour. No less than 43 per cent of the adult male population is away at work in South Africa at any one time.[28]

Basutoland's most urgent needs at present are an extension
of the soil conservation programme and the development of its
only other available resource – water. A recent Economic Survey
Mission recommended a hydrological survey as 'an urgent
necessity'.[29] It suggested that Basutoland ought to be able to
sell both water and hydro-electric power to the neighbouring
areas of South Africa.

Swaziland is smaller than the other two Territories and
potentially the richest of the three. It is about the size of Wales
and contains some 275,000 people of whom about 9,000 are
Europeans. It is unlike the other two countries in that there are
considerable areas of land in European ownership and that the
economy is based on the exploitation of minerals rather than
agriculture. About 45 per cent of the land area is in European
ownership.

The climate and soils are much more favourable for agriculture than in the other two territories and a variety of crops are
grown. There is a considerable export of sugar, butter, meat and
wood, but overwhelmingly the most important export is asbestos. In addition to asbestos there are untapped resources of
iron ore and coal, both of which could be exploited if communications were improved.

All three High Commission Territories are close and dependent neighbours of South Africa but remain a British responsibility. In the past they have suffered from neglect just
as the African areas of the Union have suffered, and little money
has been spent on them. The appointment of the recent Economic Survey Mission provides some evidence that the Government
intends to remedy this state of affairs.

The Mission approached its task 'with the question whether
there are any development projects which could be started
promptly and carried through within the next decade or so –
projects which could carry each Territory well on the way to
becoming a viable economic unit.' The Mission's recommendations would, if adopted, 'make the attainment of this goal a
near certainty in the case of Swaziland, a reasonable probability
in the case of the Bechuanaland Protectorate and a possibility
in the case of Basutoland . . .'[30]

The successful development of the High Commission Terri-

tories as envisaged by the Mission depends on two essentials;
money made available by Britain and cooperation with South
Africa.

Already the three countries are economically dependent on
South Africa. To develop them successfully would mean that
economic relations between South Africa and the Territories
'must become more numerous and complex.'[31] The political
implications of this – on all sides – have yet to be worked out.

Notes on Chapter 12 and Chapter 13

1. About twenty still exist in the Cape Province. The estimated total number still alive is about 55,000, scattered over Bechuanaland, S.W. Africa, and Angola, with a few in the Rhodesias and the Union. Most of them – 31,000 – live in Bechuanaland.

2. Note on Racial Terminology in South Africa.

   (a) 'Whites' and 'Europeans' are usually synonymous. However, some use 'Europeans' for English-speakers to distinguish them from 'Boers'. It is probably best to stick to 'Whites'.

   (b) People of negroid racial origin are referred to officially as 'Bantu'. This is now used in preference to 'Native', as the latter implies that the Whites have less right to be in the country. To call black South Africans 'Africans' is to stamp the speaker or writer as a 'liberal'. Afrikaans-speaking Whites, particularly, object to this as they now refer to themselves, not as Boers, but as 'Afrikaners' – which in English means 'Africans'.

   (c) Coloured – people of mixed racial origins.

   (d) Asiatics – mainly Indians.

3. About 50 per cent of Dutch origin.

   27 per cent of German origin.

   18 per cent of French origin.

   5 per cent of others. (Mainly Huguenots, Protestant refugees from Catholic France.)

4. Ian Laing, 'Tragic South Africa', *Sunday Times*, 5 Jan. 1958.

5. *State of the Union. Year Book for South Africa 1958*, p. 59.

6. *The Afrikaners' Share in Business 1957*:

   Commerce 25 per cent, Finance 11 per cent, Industry 6 per cent, Mining only 5 per cent, ibid., p. 59.

7.   5 Europeans to Natives
     6 Europeans to Asians
    80 Europeans to Coloured
   100 Coloured to Asians
   566 Coloured to Natives

J. H. Wellington. *Southern Africa*, Vol. II, 1955.

8. Geo. Findlay, *Miscegenation*, 1936.

9. Western Cape. Durban/Pinetown. Southern Transvaal and Port Elizabeth.

10. J. H. Wellington, op. cit., Vol. I. p. 42.

11. ibid., Vol. II, pp. xvii – xviii.

12. H. C. Brookfield. 'Some Geographical Implications of the Apartheid and Partnership Policies in Southern Africa'. Article in the Institute of British Geographers' *Transactions and Papers*, 1957, p. 232.

13. Summary of the Report of the Commission for the Socio-Economic Development of the Bantu Areas within the Union of South Africa (The Tomlinson Commission) U.G. 61/1955.

14. *Tomlinson Report*, p. 47.

15. *Tomlinson Report*, p. 51.

16. Between 3 and 4 million people.

17. *Tomlinson Report*, p. 29.

18. See 'Lines of European Development' on Map 27.

19. Both natural increase and migration.

20. *Tomlinson Report*, p. 108.

21. Van Renan and Brandt, *Eighteenth Century Explorers*, quoted by Michael Scott in *Shadow over Africa*, 1950, p. 4.

22. The Native Tribes of South West Africa and their Treatment by Germany. *H.M.S.O.*, 1918, quoted ibid., p. 4.

23. C. Arden-Clarke, 'South-West Africa, the Union and the United Nations', Article in, *African Affairs*, Jan. 1960. p. 27.

24. Paul Rohrbach, quoted by M. Scott, op. cit., p. 5.

25. The Act empowered the King in Council, on address from both Houses of the Union Parliament, to transfer the

territories to the Union subject to certain conditions designed for the protection of native rights.

26. See Chapter 15, *Basutoland, Bechuanaland and Swaziland; Report of an Economic Survey Mission*, H.M.S.O., 1960.
27. ibid., p. 53.
28. ibid., p. 226.
29. ibid., p. 255.
30. ibid., p. 12.
31. ibid., p. 12.
  See also M. Cole, *South Africa*, 1961.

Conclusion

When trouble breaks out in any part of Africa we usually generalize about it as if one part of the continent was much like any other part. Anarchy in the Congo, for example, was used to justify opposing viewpoints for different territories with different problems. We hear on the one hand that the African is 'unable to rule himself' and on the other that all colonial rule is absolutely wicked. Neither is true, even for the Congo.

We have now seen enough of the variety of Africa to realize that generalizations can be dangerous. Differences in climate, resources, racial types, social systems, economic development, and the rate and type of political progress are greater than we should find in Europe. There is no *one* Africa and no widespread sense of the need for African unity.* There are local loyalties and local problems, only some of which exist throughout the continent.

It is a truism to say that Africa is changing, but the picture of a uniform 'wind of change' is a false one. The pace of change varies as much as the scenery, and is producing even greater contrasts than before in some areas: the contrasts of modern chain stores and tin-roofed one-man shops, of university education and illiteracy, of prosperous farms and run-down subsistence holdings or of 'one man, one vote' and continuing dictatorship.

Everyone wants freedom these days and everyone has a vaguely defined desire for a better life. The two are not always complementary, however; nor do they always mean the same things. In South Africa the black Africans are certainly not 'free' but many are materially better off than they would be if

---

*Except among intellectuals and at the highest political level, as seen in the formation of the Organization of African Unity, on which *all* of independent Africa is represented.

they lived in any other part of the continent. In Rhodesia, Europeans want freedom from Whitehall and Africans from white political control. In Uganda, some Africans want freedom from Asian 'economic domination' as much as they want political independence. Pan-Africanists want not only independence but freedom from the boundaries of the colonial past.

It seems, then, that for a long time to come Africa will be divided in all sorts of ways, as indeed we might expect any other thirty or forty independent states to be. And yet, on reflection, it seems extraordinary that such a statement needs to be made at all. The countries of Europe have had contact and some understanding for centuries and are only now groping towards a wider unity. Why should we expect to find similarities rather than differences in a vast continent whose peoples are only now beginning to have close contact with each other?

The statement needs to be made, I think, because we all tend to be over-sensitive about skin colour and to feel that there must be something in common between men because they are black even more than because they are human. It leads us to be surprised at the differences and to be constantly in danger of falling back into the trap of assuming that they do not exist.

In spite of differences, however, there will still be the uniting themes which have been forced on Africa by Europe – the Bandung themes of anti-racialism, anti-colonialism, and poverty. These will present a continuing challenge to Europeans and to Europe as long as they exist anywhere in Africa. The first theme of racialism needs no emphasis but it may, perhaps, be profitable to look more closely at colonialism and poverty.

Colonialism, you will say, is on the way out. As one writer has recently put it,

European administrators are packing their bags. They are having a last look around the compounds with the whitewashed stones and the tropical flowers, the orderly district offices, the cool and old-fashioned bungalows. . . . History, having irrevocably left its mark on a changing African scene, has taken a new turn. . . .[1]

Two things need to be said about this sort of view. First,

there are still many parts of Africa, including British Africa, where colonial-type rule is strongly entrenched. Second, and perhaps more important, the suspicion of some form of 'neo-colonialism' is likely to endure for longer than the continuance of colonial rule itself. This implies a hyper-sensitivity on the part of newly emergent states about the good intentions of European countries. It may make even well-intentioned policies misunderstood. In particular, Europeans need to be wary of making their own definitions of 'independence'.

It was suggested recently in the House of Lords that Britain must 'ensure' African independence by teaching Africans not to be communists. 'We can reasonably conclude,' said Lord Twining, 'that the great majority of Africans are not enamoured with communist ideology; but they are susceptible to communist methods, and may find themselves unwittingly entrapped by them'.[2] If we go to Africa to teach *against* communism rather than *for* and *with* Africa we shall find an increasing resentment against the continuance of paternalism and quite possibly end up with the situation we most wanted to avoid.

Racialism and colonialism are largely challenges to Europe. Poverty is a joint challenge to Europe and Africa alike.

It was the experience of European rule which 'opened up' Africa and made the people of this continent of isolation and difficulty aware of both the possibility and the desirability of material progress. Self-interest and morality alike dictate that the interest of Europe in the elimination of poverty should not end with European rule. Self-interest dictates it, not because of the Cold War, but because there can be no peace in a world where the gap between the rich countries and the poor countries is increasing rather than decreasing and where the aspirations of the poor are becoming increasingly greater than the possibility of their fulfilment. Morality dictates it for those who believe that a common humanity implies a common responsibility.

For Europe this means a willingness to provide the trained men and the money (but above all the money) necessary to help promote economic growth, and to do so on a scale large enough to narrow the gap between aspiration and fulfilment. Already in some countries there is just no margin to spare for further economic progress unless help comes from outside or standards are further depressed for the sake of future generations. In Tanganyika, for example, taxation already absorbs some 20 per cent of total money incomes, and this produces only between £2 and £3 per head per annum. As the World Bank Report puts it:

> Development ... could benefit greatly from increased grants from the outside world and from external loans bearing low rates of interest, long repayment periods or liberal periods of grace before service becomes due ...[3]

The challenge to Africa is no less important. It means a willingness to change cherished ways and institutions, a willingness to experiment, to learn, and to wait for results. Above all it means a willingness to co-operate both within and between countries. Such cooperation might yet overcome the limitations of boundaries imposed by European rule and produce a much more real sense of 'Africa' than at present exists.

Notes to Conclusion

1. D. Apter, *The Political Kingdom in Uganda*, 1961, p.3
2. Speech in House of Lords, 8 November 1961. Reported by British Information Service, Kampala, 10 November 1961.
3. op. cit. p. 4.

Index

Some other Penguin and Pelican books
are described on the following pages

Primitive Government

Lucy Mair

We take so much for granted the familiar forms of government –
parliament, cabinet, ministries, law courts, and local
authorities – that we are apt to forget which features constitute the
essential elements of rule. These become clearer when we study
how government has evolved to suit the needs of family, tribe,
nation, and even empire.

Dr Mair has carried out field work on various widely differing
systems which, in spite of the imposition of colonial rule, still in
part obtain in East Africa. In these primitive societies it would
appear that concepts of law and government were already
understood and developed. In fact Dr Mair contends, contrary to
some previous opinions, that no known society exists without
them, even though their forms may be rudimentary.

Some such systems are quite outside the experience of western
readers. For instance, an apparent anarchy may prove, on
examination, to be in reality a well-ordered kind of government.
In one society political responsibility is diffused throughout the
whole; in another men have built up a kingdom which could be
compared with those of medieval Europe.

In this survey of the way in which government is conducted
without modern technical equipment, Dr Mair throws much new
light on its historical evolution.

Human Groups

W. J. H. Sprott

This book deals with 'face-to-face' relationships. These occur in relatively permanent groups, such as the family, the village, and the neighbourhood. Some of the studies which have been made of such groups are described. There has also been a great deal of experimental work done on the way in which people behave in artificial groups set up in the psychological laboratory, and a general review is given of such work and of the principal findings in the study of 'group dynamics'. An account is also given of groups of a more temporary nature, such as crowds, prison communities, and brain-washing meetings. These studies are relevant to the meaning of the expression 'Man is a social animal'. The author shows that man derives his specifically human nature from his social relationships, and discusses the present-day problem of satisfying social needs in a world of impersonal contacts. The dangers of over-socialization are also pointed out.

United Nations: Piety, Myth, and Truth

Andrew Boyd

'Certainly the most entertainingly informative account of the U.N.'s political history in print today' – *Sunday Times*

Against the tumultuous background of world news a clear and comprehensive account of the United Nations Organization is of lasting value. In this Pelican (formerly a Penguin Special which has been partially re-written and revised) Andrew Boyd of *The Economist* traces the growth of U.N.O. over the years since the San Francisco Conference of 1945, by way of Korea, Suez, Lebanon, and Laos to Katanga. Although the organization has frequently come under heavy fire, many people are ignorant of its true nature. Its record in politics provides powerful ammunition for the author's final plea for commitment to U.N.O.

'A lucid, exciting, and scrupulously exact assessment of the world body . . . a must for anybody seeking a fresh appraisal of the U.N.'s achievements, potentialities and dangers' – *Observer*

In Defence of Politics

Bernard Crick

'One of the most thoughtful products of the political dialogues of the London School of Economics since the great days of Tawney, Dalton, Wallas, and Hobhouse. Its sobriety, liberal spirit, and toughness of mind are rare qualities in any political work' – *Guardian*

At a time of brittle cynicism about the activities of politicians, this essay, which has been specially revised for Penguins, makes 'an attempt to justify politics in plain words by saying what it is'. In a civilized community, which is no mere tribe, the establishment among rival groups and interests of political order – of agreed rules for the game – marks the birth of freedom. In spite of the compromises, deals, half-measures, and bargains which prompt impatient idealists to regard politics as a dirty word – indeed, because of them – the negotiating processes of politics remain the only tested alternative to government by outright coercion.

'Original and profound. It is hard to think of anyone interested in politics at any level who would not benefit by reading it' – Max Beloff in the *Daily Telegraph*

The Economic History of World Population

Carlo M. Cipolla

This book presents a global view of the demographic and economic development of mankind.

Professor Cipolla has deliberately adopted a new point of view and has tried to trace the history of the great trends in population and wealth which have affected mankind as a whole. For it would have been inadequate to regard such a global history as being merely the sum total of national economic histories in abridged form.

Among the massive problems that face the human race the author emphasizes the demographic explosion, the economic backwardness of vast areas, the spread of industrial revolution and of technical knowledge. Whilst the theoretical approach can help our analysis of these problems, Professor Cipolla believes that they can only be wholly grasped and solved when they are studied in their full historical perspective.

The Theory and Practice of Communism

R. N. Carew Hunt

'This is the best short account of Marxism and its Russian consequences written from a highly critical standpoint that has come my way' – Edward Crankshaw in the *Observer*

R. N. Carew Hunt has come to be recognized as one of the greatest western authorities on communism. This concise and critical study of Marxism and its interpretation in practice has quickly gained the standing of a classic. The author clearly demonstrates that modern Marxism is a synthesis, in which the basic creed of Karl Marx and Engels has been tailored by Lenin and Stalin to fit the twentieth century. In its analysis of the relationship and the contrasts between Marx's predictions and the policies of the communist governments of today the book provides an excellent outline of the institutions and events which have helped to shape the map of the contemporary world – the Communist League, the First and Second Internationals, the Russian Revolution, and developments both inside and outside Russia between the time of Lenin and Khrushchev.

Geography of World Affairs

J. P. Cole

Day after day more and more places are mentioned in the
newspapers, on the radio, and on television. It may be possible to
follow world affairs and world problems without knowing anything
about Queen Maud Land or Okinawa, Ruanda and Burundi or
Surinam, but few people have more than a vague impression even
of such important places as Formosa, Turkey, or Venezuela.

This book, which has now been completely revised and brought up
to date, sets out to help the reader who is not a specialist in
geography to find his way about the world and to provide him with
facts about the location, population, size, and activities of the more
important countries in it. Most of the material in this book is
geographical in nature, but many questions cannot be
considered, even from a purely geographical viewpoint, without
reference to history, politics, and economics.

The Penguin African Library

'Penguin's . . . breaking new ground in politics on a scale unmatched since their spate of Penguin Specials on the eve of the last war' – *Financial Times*

'Penguin Books are to be congratulated on making the first serious attempt to provide the man in the street with the authoritative background information and responsible comment on every aspect of the continent's affairs' – *Oxford Mail*

Titles already published in the series are:

For a complete list of books available please write to Penguin Books whose address can be found on the back of the title page